Student Cookbook

Easy & Affordable Eats

Table of Contents

Introduction 10

Chapter 1: Basics of Cooking 13
    Flaming Passion, Not Your Dinner 13
    Sharp Mind, Sharper Knives 14
    Tools of the Trade 14
    Technique Talk 15
    Basic Tools: The Fellowship of the Essential Gadgets 15
    Pantry Staples: Your Budget-Friendly Grocery List 17

Chapter 2: Quick Breakfasts 19
    Overnight Oats Variations 20
        1. Easy Rolled Oats 20
        2. Peanut Butter & Banana Overnight Oats 21
        3. Berry Blast Overnight Oats 22
    Smoothie Bowls & Recipes 23
        1. Classic Fruit Medley Smoothie Bowl 23
        2. Tropical Paradise Smoothie Bowl 24
        3. Chocolate Dream Smoothie Bowl 25
    Breakfast Burritos 26
        1. Classic Breakfast Burrito 26
        2. Spinach and Feta Burrito 27
        3. Sausage and Hash Brown Burrito 28
        4. Black Bean and Avocado Burrito 29
        5. Simple Avocado Toast: 30
    Omelets 31
        1. Classic Cheese Omelet 31

- 2. Spinach and Feta Omelet ... 32
- 3. Mushroom and Onion Omelet ... 33
- Banana Pancakes ... 34
- Yogurt & Granola Parfait ... 35
- Toasted Breakfast Sandwich ... 36
- Quickie Quesadilla ... 37
- Cereal & Milk Boost ... 38

Chapter 3: Easy Lunches ... 39

- Salad in a Jar ... 40
  - 1. Classic Tuna Pasta Salad ... 40
  - 2. Refreshing Chickpea Salad ... 41
  - 3. Zesty Asian Noodle Salad ... 42
- Wraps and Sandwiches: Different Fillings and Ideas ... 43
  - 1. Veggie & Hummus Wrap ... 43
  - 2. Tuna Salad Sandwich ... 44
  - 3. Egg & Avocado Wrap ... 45
  - 4. Chicken Caesar Wrap ... 46
  - 5. BBQ Chicken Sandwich ... 47
- Quick stir-fries ... 48
  - 1. Chicken & Bell Pepper Stir Fry ... 48
  - 2. Beef & Broccoli Stir Fry ... 49
  - 3. Shrimp & Snow Pea Stir Fry ... 50
  - 4. Tofu & Mixed Veggie Stir Fry ... 51
  - 5. Pork & Green Bean Stir Fry ... 52
- Rice Bowls ... 53
  - 1. Chicken Teriyaki Rice Bowl ... 53
  - 2. Veggie & Egg Rice Bowl ... 54
  - 3. Spicy Chicken Rice Bowl ... 55
  - 4. Sweet & Sour Tofu Rice Bowl ... 56
  - 5. Beef & Broccoli Rice Bowl ... 57
- DIY Instant Noodles in a Jar ... 58
  - 1. Spicy Chicken Instant Noodles in a Jar ... 58
  - 2. Miso Veggie Instant Noodles in a Jar ... 60

Chapter 4: Simple Dinners ... 61

- One-pot pasta dishes ... 61
  - 1. Garlic Parmesan Spaghetti ... 63

   2. Creamy Tomato and Basil Pasta 64
   3. One-Pot Pesto Pasta 65
   4. One-Pot Chili Mac 66
   5. One-Pot Lemon Garlic Pasta 67
   6. One-Pot Creamy Mushroom Pasta 68
   7. One-Pot Taco Pasta 69
   8. One-Pot Broccoli Alfredo Pasta 70
   9. One-Pot Cajun Spice Pasta 71
   10. One-Pot Sun-dried Tomato and Spinach Pasta 72
   11. One-Pot Greek Pasta 73
   12. One-Pot Pesto and Pea Pasta 74
   13. One-Pot Tomato Basil Pasta 75

Sheet Pan Meals 76
   1. Lemon Herb Chicken & Potatoes 76
   2. Spiced Chickpea & Veggie Tray 77
   3. Honey Mustard Salmon & Asparagus 78
   4. Teriyaki Tofu & Broccoli 79
   5. BBQ Sausage & Mixed Veggies 80
   6. Garlic Parmesan Shrimp & Green Beans 81
   7. Balsamic Chicken & Root Veggies 82
   8. Spicy Sausage & Bell Peppers 83
   9. Rosemary Lemon Tilapia & Zucchini 84
   10. Cumin Roasted Chickpea & Sweet Potato 85
   11. BBQ Tempeh & Broccoli 86
   12. Greek Lemon Oregano Tofu & Tomatoes 87

Quick Curries 88
   1. Chickpea Coconut Curry 90
   2. Quick Chicken Curry 91
   3. Simple Veggie Curry 92
   4. Quick Beef Curry 93
   5. Lamb Keema Curry 94
   6. Turkey & Spinach Curry 95
   7. Pork & Apple Curry 96
   8. Chicken & Bell Pepper Curry 97
   9. Creamy Tomato Chicken Curry 98
   10. Spicy Beef & Potato Curry 99
   11. Pork Vindaloo Curry 100
   12. Lamb & Apricot Curry 101

Tacos & fajitas 102

1. Classic Beef Tacos	102
2. Chicken Fajitas	103
3. Veggie Tacos	104
4. Shrimp Fajitas	105
5. Spicy Pork Tacos	106
6. Veggie Fajitas	107
Homemade pizza	108
1. Classic Margherita Pizza	108
2. BBQ Chicken Tortilla Pizza	109
3. Veggie Delight Pizza	110
4. Pesto & Feta Tortilla Pizza	111
5. Pepperoni & Olive Pizza	112

Chapter 5: Snacks & Sides — 113

DIY Trail Mix	114
Veggies & dip	115
1. Simple Hummus	115
2. Tzatziki	116
3. Garlic & Herb Cream Cheese Dip	117
4. Spicy Salsa	118
5. Avocado Guacamole	119
6. Cheesy Queso Dip	120
7. Peanut Butter Yogurt Dip	121
Quesadillas	122
1. Classic Cheese Quesadilla	122
2. Chicken & Pepper Quesadilla	123
3. Spinach & Feta Quesadilla	124
4. Black Bean & Corn Quesadilla	125
Baked sweet potato fries	126
1. Classic Baked Sweet Potato Fries	126
2. Spicy Baked Sweet Potato Fries	127

Chapter 6: Weekend Meals — 128

Easy Chili	128
1. Classic Beef Chili	129
2. Chicken Chili	130
Basic Stews & Soups	131
1. Simple Vegetable Soup	131

    2. Classic Chicken Noodle Soup 132
    3. Tomato Basil Soup 133
    4. Lentil Soup 134
    5. Potato Leek Soup 135
    6. Broccoli Cheddar Soup 136
    7. Minestrone Soup 137
    8. Beef Barley Soup 138

DIY Burgers 139
    1. Basic Beef Burger 139
    2. Spicy Chicken Burger 140
    3. Simple Veggie Burger 141
    4. Cheesy Beef Burger 142
    5. Herb Chicken Burger 143
    6. Mushroom Veggie Burger 144
    7. BBQ Beef Burger 145
    8. Asian-style Chicken Burger 146

Casseroles 147
    1. Classic Tuna Pasta Casserole 147
    2. Cheesy Potato & Sausage Casserole 148
    3. Veggie Rice Casserole 149

Slow Cooker Recipes 150
    1. Basic Pulled Pork 150
    2. Veggie Cacciatore 151
    3. Chicken Curry 152
    4. Beef Stew 153
    5. Bean Chili 154
    6. Creamy Garlic Chicken 155
    7. Spaghetti Bolognese 156
    8. Sausage & Bean Casserole 157
    9. Coconut Lentil Curry 158
    10. BBQ Pulled Chicken 159
    11. Creamy Mushroom & Chicken 160

Curries from Scratch 161
    1. Chicken Tikka Masala 162
    2. Lamb Rogan Josh 164
    3. Beef Vindaloo 165
    4. Vegetable Korma 166
    5. Thai Green Chicken Curry 167

6. Thai Red Curry with Beef 168
7. Moroccan Lamb Curry 169
8. Japanese Curry with Pork 170

Chapter 7: Fakeaway - Your Fave UK Takeaways Reimagined 171

1. Fernando's Fiery Grilled Chicken 172
2. Cheeky Chicken Wings 173
3. Spicy Bean Burger (Veggie option) 174
4. Peri-Peri Corn on the Cob 175

Wok-a-mama's 176
1. Wok-a-mama's Classic Ramen 176
2. Quickie Stir-fry Noodles 177
3. Spicy Coconut Curry 178
4. Tofu Teriyaki Bowl 179

Mackie D's 180
1. Mackie's Classic Burger 180
2. Crispy Chicken Sandwich 181
3. Mackie's Veggie Delight Wrap 182
4. Mackie's Apple Pie Turnover 183

Starbeans 184
1. Starbeans Classic Brew 184
2. Starbeans Iced Coffee Blend 185
3. Starbeans Chocolate Dream 186
4. Starbeans Coconut Bliss 187
5. Starbeans Honey Almond Delight 188
6. Starbeans Herbal Fusion 189

Pret a Almost's 190
1. Classic Chicken Caesar Wrap 190
2. Tuna Nicoise Sandwich 191
3. Vegetarian Avo & Hummus Baguette 192
4. Vegan Falafel & Tzatziki Wrap 193
5. Pret a Almost's Porridge with Berries & Honey 194

GFC 195
1. GFC's Classic Fried Chicken Drumstick 195
2. GFC's Crispy Chicken Burger 197
3. GFC's Sticky BBQ Wings 198

Chapter 8: Airfryer Adventures — 199

Crispy Snacks — 200
   1. AirFried Crunchy Chicken Strips — 200
   2. Golden Brown Mozzarella Sticks — 201
   3. Zesty Zucchini Fries — 202
   4. AirCrisped Potato Wedges — 203
   5. Crunchy AirFried Chickpeas — 204
   6. AirFryer Stuffed Jalapeños — 205
   7. AirBaked Apple Chips — 206

Main Dishes — 207
   1. AirFryer Lemon Herb Chicken — 207
   2. Quick AirFryer Pita Pizzas — 208
   3. Airfryer Veggie Frittata — 209
   4. AirFried Asian Glazed Meatballs — 210
   5. AirFryer BBQ Chicken Drumsticks — 211
   6. AirFryer Crispy Tofu Bites — 212
   7. AirFryer Stuffed Bell Peppers — 213
   8. AirFryer Fish 'n Chips — 214

Veggies & Sides — 215
   1. AirFryer Parmesan Zucchini Chips — 215
   2. AirFryer Garlic Baby Potatoes — 216
   3. AirFryer Asparagus with Lemon Zest — 217
   4. AirFryer Sweet Corn with Paprika Butter — 218

Chapter 9: Desserts & Treats — 219

Mug Cakes — 220
   1. Classic Chocolate Mug Cake — 220
   2. Vanilla Berry Mug Cake — 221

No-Bake Cookies — 222
   1. Peanut Butter Oat Balls — 222
   2. Chocolate Coconut Drops — 223

Fruit Salad Variations — 224
   1. Citrus Burst Bowl — 224
   2. Melon Medley — 225
   3. Exotic Fruit Fiesta — 226
   4. Berry Bliss Salad — 227
   5. Pomegranate & Pear Pleasure — 228

DIY Frozen Yogurt — 229

    1. Classic Vanilla Bean Frozen Yogurt _____ 229
    2. Berry Blast Frozen Yogurt _____ 230
    3. Tropical Mango & Coconut Frozen Yogurt _____ 231
    4. Chocolate Swirl Frozen Yogurt _____ 232
  Simple Fruit Crisps _____ 233
    1. Classic Apple Crisp _____ 233
    2. Berry Medley Crisp _____ 234

Chapter 10: Budgeting & Shopping Tips _____ 235
  How to Make a Meal Plan _____ 235
  Shopping on a Budget: Navigating the Grocery Store Jungle __ 237
  Seasonal Shopping: The UK's Orchestra of Harvests _____ 240
  Storing Food Correctly: The Art of the Culinary Librarian ____ 242

Chapter 11: Scaling & Meal Prepping _____ 244
  Freezing and Reheating 101: Maximising Meal Potential _____ 246
  The Reheat Rundown: Dos, Don'ts, and Precautions _____ 247
  Batch Cooking Brilliance: A Crash Course in Culinary Efficiency _____ 249

Appendices _____ 253
  Nutritional Guidelines: Building Blocks for a Balanced Diet __ 253

Glossary: Decoding Cooking Lingo _____ 255

Substitution Chart: Swapping in a Pinch ____ 257

Introduction

Welcome to Your Culinary Quest, Fellow Food Fanatics!

Hey there, future mastermind of the microwave, conqueror of the cooker, and sultan of the stovetop! Feeling overwhelmed about the prospect of feeding yourself? Fear not! We're here to help you navigate the sometimes stormy, sometimes sunny, but always scrumptious shores of student cooking.

Imagine: It's a crisp autumn evening, and while everyone else is ordering takeout, you're whipping up a delectable, wallet-friendly dish that has your housemates peering into your kitchen, wondering if they've accidentally roomed with Gordon Ramsay's protégé.

That's the dream, right? This book is your trusty vessel to get you there. And we promise, no complex culinary lingo or ingredients you can't pronounce. From breakfast blitzes to dinner delights, here's what you can expect:

Purpose of the Book: At its heart, this guide is here to prove that delicious and nutritious can indeed go hand-in-hand with affordable and doable. Say goodbye to beans-on-toast every night (unless that's your jam) and say hello to a world where your meals are the envy of every flatmate and friend.

Basics of Cooking: Not all heroes wear capes; some wear aprons. Before we dive deep, we'll cover the foundational cooking techniques, ensuring your kitchen adventures are both safe and successful. Think of this as the 'learning to crawl before you walk' section.

Chapters 1 to 3: Equip your culinary arsenal. From tools to ingredients, and kickstarting your day with power-packed breakfasts to mid-day meal marvels, we're laying the foundation stone of your gastronomic journey.

Chapters 4 to 6: Elevate your evenings and weekends. Here, we venture into the realm of hearty dinners and relaxed weekend meals. The goal? Dishes that soothe the soul after a gruelling day of lectures or a marathon study session.

Chapter 7: Craving takeout? We're recreating UK's finest without the hefty price tag. Dive into our 'Fakeaway' section and discover how your favourite takeaways can come alive in your kitchen.

Chapter 8: Airfryer aficionados, assemble! If you've got one of these modern marvels, or are contemplating an investment, this chapter will guide you through snacks, main dishes, sides, and even some sweet treats—all with less oil and fuss.

Chapter 9: For the sweet-toothed scholars among you, our desserts section promises indulgences that are both simple and sensational. Be it a quick mug cake or a refreshing fruit salad, we've got you covered.

Chapters 10 & 11: Behind every great chef is a well-organised kitchen and plan. We delve into the arts of budgeting, shopping, meal prepping, and ensuring that your efforts in the kitchen yield dividends for days, if not weeks!

Conclusion: Beyond just recipes and techniques, we hope to instil in you a love for the culinary arts. Because, at the end of the day, cooking is more than just about feeding oneself—it's an act of self-care, creativity, and often, camaraderie.

Ready to embark on this delectable journey? Flip the page, and let's get the culinary ball rolling!

Chapter 1

Basics of Cooking

Flaming Passion, Not Your Dinner

Controlling Your Heat: Just like juggling study, sleep, and social life, heat management in cooking is all about balance. Too much and you're burning bridges (and your food). Too little, and well, you're not really cooking.

- High Heat: Perfect for stir-fries and searing. It's like pulling an all-nighter – fast, intense, and over before you know it.
- Medium Heat: Ideal for everyday cooking, like frying eggs or pancakes. It's the lecture you pay half-attention to but still manage to jot down notes.
- Low Heat: Great for simmering sauces or stews. Think of it as the slow, consistent study session for a major exam. Patience brings flavor!

Sharp Mind, Sharper Knives

Knife Skills 101: Owning a sharp knife is like having a fully charged laptop during finals week – incredibly useful and a total game-changer. But with great power comes great responsibility.

- The Grip: Hold your knife like you'd clasp a handshake with your future employer – firm and confident. Thumb and forefinger grasping the blade, while the other fingers wrap around the handle.
- The Claw: Protect those digits! Curl the fingers of your free hand, guiding the knife against the knuckles while slicing. Picture playing a very careful game of "The Floor is Lava," but with your fingers and a knife.

Tools of the Trade

Essentials to Kickstart: If your kitchen were a party, these tools would be the DJ, the dance floor, and the mood lighting, setting the vibes right!

- The Saucy Pan: Non-stick pans are the Swiss army knives of the kitchen world. From sunrise scrambled eggs to midnight pancakes, they've got you covered.
- Pot-tastic: A decent-sized pot is like that one friend who's ready for any plans, be it an impromptu road trip or a Netflix binge. Essential for pasta, soups, or the legendary ramen.
- Mix-a-lot Bowl: A sturdy mixing bowl is like your study group: accommodating, reliable, and vital for last-minute prep – or in this case, salads and cake

batters.

Technique Talk

Stirring & Flipping: Like trying to decipher your lecturer's handwriting or understand abstract art, these techniques can be elusive but are crucial to master.

- Stirring: The age-old clockwise, counterclockwise debate. The reality? Just ensure everything gets a good whirl, like rotating study topics to keep things fresh.
- Flipping: Be it pancakes or omelets, the trick is in the wrist. It's like perfecting the frisbee throw. Start with a little enthusiasm and a lot of practice.

With these basics, you're set to begin your culinary university. Remember, like any skill, cooking is a mix of knowledge, practice, and those inevitable "Oops! Wasn't supposed to do that" moments. Embrace them and enjoy the edible outcomes!

Basic Tools: The Fellowship of the Essential Gadgets

"Ahoy, culinary adventurers! Just like a knight wouldn't venture into a battle without their sword, or a wizard without their wand, a kitchen warrior needs their trusty tools. But fear not! You won't need a treasure chest of gold to equip your kitchen for the culinary quests ahead."

- The Non-Stick Pan: Your trusty sidekick! Whether you're summoning breakfast or a late-night snack, this fella ensures minimal food-sticking tragedies and

easy cleaning.
- The Multipurpose Pot: Like the reliable friend who's always game for any plan, this pot's great for pasta nights, soup soirees, or the legendary instant ramen revival.
- Wooden Spoon: Think of it as the Gandalf of your Middle-Earth kitchen. Ideal for stirring, tasting, and (occasionally) pointing dramatically while you announce the next recipe.
- Chef's Knife: The Excalibur of the kitchen. Slicing, dicing, chopping, and occasionally pretending you're on a cooking show – this blade does it all.
- Mixing Bowl: The container of culinary creativity. Essential for throwing together salads, marinating proteins, or attempting homemade brownies for that special someone (or just yourself, we don't judge).
- Measuring Cups & Spoons: Because sometimes cooking is like that precise chemistry experiment where accuracy can mean the difference between deliciousness and disaster.
- Can Opener: Your gateway to affordable ingredients. Canned beans, tomatoes, and fruits are all behind these metallic gates.
- Colander/Strainer: Perfect for when you're trying to separate the solids from the liquids, much like skimming lecture notes before an exam.
- Spatula: The unsung hero for flipping pancakes, scrambling eggs, or scraping out the last bit of peanut butter from the jar.

Pantry Staples: Your Budget-Friendly Grocery List

"Okay, kitchen knights, your armory is set. Now, what about the arsenal? The ingredients! The budget-friendly magic potions and elixirs that'll transform your meals from 'meh' to 'more please!' Here's what to keep stocked for tasty, wallet-friendly wizardry."

Grains & Pasta:

- Rice: Whether it's white, brown, or wild, it's a blank canvas for a plethora of dishes.
- Pasta: Spaghetti, penne, or macaroni – quick to cook and oh so versatile.

Canned Goods:

- Beans: Black, kidney, or chickpeas – a protein-packed addition to salads, curries, and soups.
- Tomatoes: The base for sauces, curries, and chilis.
- Tuna or Sardines: For quick sandwiches, salads, or pastas.

Spices & Condiments:

- Salt & Pepper: The Batman & Robin of seasoning. Always have them around.
- Oil (like olive or vegetable): For cooking and simple dressings.
- Soy Sauce & Hot Sauce: When you need a flavor kick without the fuss.

Dairy & Alternatives:

- Milk or Plant-based alternatives: For your cereals,

teas, or creamy dishes.
- Eggs: The Swiss Army knife of the food world. Boil, fry, scramble, or bake!

Frozen Goods:
- Vegetables: They last longer and are often pre-chopped. Talk about convenience!
- Berries: For smoothies or a quick snack.

Baking Basics (for when you're feeling fancy):
- Flour: The foundation of pancakes, cookies, or thickening sauces.
- Sugar: To sweeten life up a bit.
- Baking Soda & Baking Powder: For the occasional baking extravaganza.

Chapter 2

Quick Breakfasts

Overnight Oats Variations

1. Easy Rolled Oats

Serves: 1

Ingredients:

- 1/2 cup rolled oats
- 2/3 cup milk (dairy or plant-based)
- 1 tablespoon sugar or any sweetener you have on hand
- Optional toppings: chopped fruit or a dollop of jam.

Steps:

1. Mix oats, milk, and sweetener in a container.
2. Let it sit in the fridge overnight.
3. In the morning, stir and add any toppings you fancy.

Alternatives:

- Texture Boost: Add a tablespoon of chia seeds before refrigerating.

2. Peanut Butter & Banana Overnight Oats

Serves: 1

Ingredients:

- 1/2 cup rolled oats
- 2/3 cup milk (dairy or plant-based)
- 1 tablespoon honey or maple syrup
- 1 tablespoon peanut butter (or any nut or seed butter available)
- 1/2 banana, sliced

Steps:

1. In a container, combine oats, milk, honey or maple syrup, and peanut butter.
2. Give it a good stir to ensure everything is mixed well.
3. Let it sit in the fridge overnight.
4. In the morning, stir again and top with banana slices.

Alternatives:

- Chocolate Delight: Add a teaspoon of cocoa powder during the mixing for a chocolaty twist.
- Nut Crunch: Sprinkle some crushed walnuts or almonds on top before eating.

3. Berry Blast Overnight Oats

Serves: 1

Ingredients:

- 1/2 cup rolled oats
- 2/3 cup milk (dairy or plant-based)
- 1 tablespoon sugar or any sweetener you have on hand
- A handful of mixed berries (like strawberries, blueberries, or raspberries)

Steps:

1. Mix oats, milk, and sweetener in a container.
2. Let it sit in the fridge overnight.
3. In the morning, give it a stir and garnish with a generous helping of mixed berries.

Alternatives:

- Exotic Twist: Swap the berries for a tropical fruit mix like mango and pineapple chunks.
- Creamy Dream: Stir in a tablespoon of yogurt in the morning for a creamier texture.

Smoothie Bowls & Recipes

1. Classic Fruit Medley Smoothie Bowl

Serves: 1

Ingredients:

- 1 cup frozen fruits (whatever's on sale or in the freezer)
- 1/2 cup milk or water
- Optional toppings: a sprinkle of oats or some sliced banana.

Steps:

1. Blend the frozen fruits with milk or water until smooth.
2. Pour into a bowl and garnish with your selected toppings.

Alternatives:

- Protein Punch: Blend in a tablespoon of peanut butter or a handful of nuts.
- Green Machine: Add a handful of spinach to the blender for a nutrient boost.

2. Tropical Paradise Smoothie Bowl

Serves: 1

Ingredients:

- 1/2 cup frozen mango chunks
- 1/2 cup frozen pineapple pieces
- 1/2 cup coconut milk or water
- Optional toppings: shredded coconut or a dash of chia seeds.

Steps:

1. Blend the mango and pineapple with coconut milk or water until creamy.
2. Empty the blend into a bowl and sprinkle with your preferred toppings.

Alternatives:

- Zesty Twist: Add a squeeze of lime juice before blending.
- Berry Blast: Top with some fresh or frozen berries for an added fruity touch.

3. Chocolate Dream Smoothie Bowl

Serves: 1

Ingredients:

- 1 banana, frozen and sliced
- 1 tablespoon cocoa powder
- 1/2 cup almond milk or water
- Optional toppings: a drizzle of honey or some chocolate shavings.

Steps:

1. Blend the banana, cocoa powder, and almond milk until it achieves a velvety texture.
2. Transfer to a bowl and finish with your choice of toppings.

Alternatives:

- Nutty Delight: Mix in a tablespoon of almond or hazelnut butter before blending.
- Red Velvet: Add a handful of frozen raspberries to the blender for a fruity and tangy twist.

Breakfast Burritos

1. Classic Breakfast Burrito

Serves: 1

Ingredients:

- 1 large tortilla wrap
- 1 egg
- 2 tablespoons grated cheese (like cheddar or mozzarella)
- Salt and pepper to taste

Steps:

1. Beat the egg in a bowl, season with salt and pepper.
2. In a pan over medium heat, scramble the egg until fully cooked.
3. Lay out the tortilla, place the scrambled egg in the center, and sprinkle with cheese.
4. Fold, roll, and enjoy immediately or let it cool to store for later.

Alternatives:

- Veggie Boost: Add some diced bell peppers or tomatoes when scrambling.
- Meat Lover: Include cooked bacon bits or sausage crumbles.

2. Spinach and Feta Burrito

Serves: 1

Ingredients:

- 1 large tortilla wrap
- 1 egg
- 1/4 cup fresh spinach, roughly chopped
- 2 tablespoons feta cheese, crumbled
- Salt and pepper to taste

Steps:

1. Beat the egg, season with salt and pepper.
2. In a pan, sauté spinach until wilted.
3. Add the beaten egg, scramble with the spinach.
4. Lay out the tortilla, add the mixture, sprinkle with feta, fold, and roll.

Alternatives:

- Add diced tomatoes or olives.
- Substitute feta with goat cheese.

3. Sausage and Hash Brown Burrito

Serves: 1

Ingredients:

- 1 large tortilla wrap
- 1 egg
- 1 small sausage link, cooked and chopped
- 1/4 cup frozen hash browns or diced potatoes
- Salt and pepper to taste

Steps:

1. Cook hash browns or potatoes in a pan.
2. Push them aside, heat the sausage.
3. Beat the egg, season, scramble in the pan.
4. Place on the tortilla, roll, and serve.

Alternatives:

- Add grilled bell peppers or onions.
- Swap sausage with bacon or ham.

4. Black Bean and Avocado Burrito

Serves: 1

Ingredients:

- 1 large tortilla wrap
- 1 egg
- 1/4 cup black beans, drained and rinsed
- 1/4 avocado, sliced
- Salt and pepper to taste

Steps:

1. Scramble the egg in a pan, season it.
2. Warm the black beans.
3. On the tortilla, spread egg, beans, and avocado slices.
4. Roll it up and dig in!

Alternatives:

- Drizzle with salsa or hot sauce.
- Sprinkle with cheese.

To Store for Later: Allow the burrito to cool down after cooking. Wrap it in foil or cling film and store it in the freezer.

To Reheat: Unwrap the burrito and microwave on high for 1-2 minutes or until heated through. For students without microwaves, the burritos can be reheated in a pan over medium heat until warm, turning occasionally.

5. Simple Avocado Toast:

Serves: 1

Ingredients:

- 2 slices of bread
- 1 ripe avocado
- Salt and pepper to taste

Steps:

1. Toast the bread.
2. Mash the avocado and spread it on the toast. Season with salt and pepper.

Alternatives:

- Eggstra Delicious: Top with a fried egg for added protein.

Omelets

1. Classic Cheese Omelet

Serves: 1

Ingredients:

- 2 eggs
- 2 tablespoons grated cheese (like cheddar or mozzarella)
- 1 tablespoon butter or oil
- Salt and pepper to taste

Steps:

1. In a bowl, whisk the eggs with salt and pepper.
2. On medium heat, warm the butter or oil in a non-stick pan.
3. Once the butter is melted or the oil is hot, pour in the beaten eggs, spreading them evenly.
4. As the eggs start to set on the bottom, sprinkle the cheese over one half.
5. Once the top is nearly set, fold the omelet in half using a spatula.
6. Serve immediately.

Alternatives:

- Herby Delight: Mix in some dried herbs like basil or oregano for added flavor.
- Spicy Twist: Add a few dashes of hot sauce or chili flakes for a kick.

2. *Spinach and Feta Omelet*

Serves: 1

Ingredients:

- 2 eggs
- 1/4 cup fresh spinach, roughly chopped
- 2 tablespoons feta cheese, crumbled
- 1 tablespoon butter or oil
- Salt and pepper to taste

Steps:

1. In a bowl, beat the eggs and season with salt and pepper.
2. Heat butter or oil on medium heat in a pan, then add the spinach, cooking until wilted.
3. Pour the beaten eggs over the spinach, allowing them to spread across the pan.
4. Once the eggs start to solidify, sprinkle the feta cheese over one side.
5. When the top is almost set, fold the omelet in half.
6. Serve hot.

Alternatives:

- Tomato Burst: Include some cherry tomatoes for a refreshing twist.
- Mediterranean Touch: Add chopped olives or a drizzle of pesto.

3. Mushroom and Onion Omelet

Serves: 1

Ingredients:

- 2 eggs
- 1/4 cup mushrooms, sliced
- 2 tablespoons onion, finely chopped
- 1 tablespoon butter or oil
- Salt and pepper to taste

Steps:

1. Whisk the eggs in a bowl, adding salt and pepper for seasoning.
2. In a pan on medium heat, melt the butter or heat the oil. Sauté the onions and mushrooms until they're soft and golden.
3. Distribute the onion and mushroom mix evenly in the pan, and pour over the beaten eggs.
4. Let the eggs set around the edges. Once the top is nearly firm, you can choose to fold the omelet in half or leave it open-faced.
5. Plate and savor!

Alternatives:

- Cheesy Goodness: Mix in some grated parmesan or cheddar before folding.
- Green Kick: Incorporate chopped bell peppers for an added crunch.

Banana Pancakes

Serves: 1

Ingredients:

- 1 ripe banana
- 2 eggs

Steps:

1. Mash the banana in a bowl.
2. Whisk in the eggs until combined.
3. Heat a non-stick pan over medium heat.
4. Pour small amounts of the mixture to make pancakes. Cook until bubbles appear on the surface, then flip and cook the other side.
5. Serve hot with whatever toppings you have, like jam or a sprinkle of sugar.

Alternatives:

- Add a sprinkle of cinnamon or cocoa powder to the mix for extra flavor.

Yogurt & Granola Parfait

Serves: 1

Ingredients:

- 1 cup yogurt (any flavor you have)
- 1/2 cup granola or muesli
- Optional: any fruit you have, like slices of banana or apple

Steps:

1. In a glass or bowl, layer yogurt and granola alternately.
2. Top with fruit slices if available.
3. Grab a spoon and enjoy!

Alternatives:

- Add a drizzle of honey or chocolate syrup for extra sweetness.

Toasted Breakfast Sandwich

Serves: 1

Ingredients:

- 2 slices of bread
- 1 egg
- 1 slice of cheese
- Optional: a slice of tomato or lettuce

Steps:

1. Cook the egg (fried or scrambled) in a pan and season with salt and pepper.
2. Toast the bread slices.
3. Place the cooked egg and cheese (and any veggies if you have them) between the bread slices.
4. Enjoy the sandwich as is, or if you're feeling fancy, heat it up a bit in the pan to melt the cheese.

Alternatives:

- Add a slice of deli meat or some leftover cooked vegetables.

Quickie Quesadilla

Serves: 1

Ingredients:

- 1 large tortilla
- 1/2 cup grated cheese

Steps:

1. Heat a pan over medium heat.
2. Sprinkle half the tortilla with cheese and fold it over.
3. Place the folded tortilla in the pan. Cook until golden brown, then flip and cook the other side.
4. Remove, let it cool for a moment, cut into wedges, and enjoy!

Alternatives:

- Add some beans, leftover veggies, or a dollop of salsa if available.

Cereal & Milk Boost

Serves: 1

Ingredients:

- 1 cup of your favorite cereal (whatever's on sale or in your cupboard)
- 1 cup milk (dairy or plant-based)

Steps:

1. Pour cereal into a bowl.
2. Add milk.
3. That's it. Seriously. Breakfast in under a minute!

Alternatives:

- Top with some chopped fruit, nuts, or a sprinkle of sugar for added flavor.

Chapter 3

Easy Lunches

Salad in a Jar

1. Classic Tuna Pasta Salad

Serves: 1

Ingredients:

- 2 tablespoons of olive oil and vinegar dressing
- 1/2 cup of cooked pasta
- 1/4 cup of canned tuna, drained
- 1/4 cup of chopped bell pepper
- 1/4 cup of canned corn, drained
- A pinch of salt and pepper

Steps:

1. Add the dressing at the bottom of the jar.
2. Layer with pasta, tuna, bell pepper, and corn.
3. Seal the jar. Shake well before eating.

Alternatives:

- Swap tuna with canned beans for a vegetarian option.
- Add some olives or feta cheese if on hand.

2. Refreshing Chickpea Salad

Serves: 1

Ingredients:

- 2 tablespoons of lemon and olive oil dressing
- 1/2 cup of canned chickpeas, drained and rinsed
- 1/4 cup of diced cucumber
- 1/4 cup of cherry tomatoes, halved
- 1 tablespoon of red onion, finely chopped (optional)
- A pinch of salt and pepper

Steps:

1. Pour the dressing into the jar.
2. Layer with chickpeas, cucumber, tomatoes, and red onion.
3. Seal the jar. Give it a shake before digging in.

Alternatives:

- Add a sprinkle of feta cheese for added flavor.
- Toss in some fresh parsley or mint if available.

3. Zesty Asian Noodle Salad

Serves: 1

Ingredients:

- 2 tablespoons of soy sauce and sesame oil dressing
- 1/2 cup of cooked ramen or any noodles
- 1/4 cup of julienned carrots
- 1/4 cup of thinly sliced bell pepper
- 1/4 cup of canned or fresh peas
- A sprinkle of sesame seeds (optional)
- A pinch of salt and pepper

Steps:

1. Add the dressing to the bottom of the jar.
2. Layer with noodles, carrots, bell pepper, and peas.
3. Seal the jar. Shake well when you're ready to eat.

Alternatives:

- Incorporate some leftover chicken or tofu for protein.
- Add a dash of chili flakes or hot sauce for a kick.

Wraps and Sandwiches: Different Fillings and Ideas

1. Veggie & Hummus Wrap

Serves: 1

Ingredients:

- 1 large tortilla wrap
- 2 tablespoons hummus
- Sliced cucumber
- Sliced bell pepper
- A handful of spinach or lettuce

Steps:

1. Spread hummus on the tortilla.
2. Add the sliced veggies and greens.
3. Roll it up, slice in half, and serve.

2. Tuna Salad Sandwich

Serves: 1

Ingredients:

- 2 slices of bread
- 1 can of tuna, drained
- 1 tablespoon mayo
- A sprinkle of salt and pepper
- Optional: lettuce or sliced tomatoes

Steps:

1. Mix the tuna with mayo, salt, and pepper.
2. Spread the tuna mix on one slice of bread.
3. Add lettuce or tomatoes if available.
4. Top with the second bread slice and enjoy.

3. Egg & Avocado Wrap

Serves: 1

Ingredients:

- 1 large tortilla wrap
- 1 boiled egg, sliced
- 1/2 avocado, sliced
- A pinch of salt and pepper

Steps:

1. Lay out the tortilla.
2. Place the egg and avocado slices in the center.
3. Season with salt and pepper.
4. Roll it up, and it's ready to eat.

4. Chicken Caesar Wrap

Serves: 1

Ingredients:

- 1 large tortilla wrap
- 1/2 cup grilled chicken, sliced (can use leftover rotisserie chicken)
- 1/4 cup lettuce, shredded
- 2 tablespoons Caesar dressing
- 1 tablespoon grated Parmesan cheese
- A sprinkle of black pepper

Steps:

1. Lay out the tortilla.
2. Spread Caesar dressing over the surface.
3. Add the sliced chicken, lettuce, and sprinkle with Parmesan and black pepper.
4. Roll it up tightly, slice in half, and serve.

Alternatives:

- Use whole wheat or spinach tortillas for a different twist.
- Add croutons for some crunch.

5. BBQ Chicken Sandwich

Serves: 1

Ingredients:

- 2 slices of bread (any kind you like)
- 1/2 cup of shredded chicken (leftovers work great)
- 3 tablespoons of BBQ sauce
- Optional: lettuce or coleslaw for added crunch
- 1 slice of cheese (like cheddar or provolone)

Steps:

1. In a bowl, mix the shredded chicken with BBQ sauce until well-coated.
2. Lay one slice of bread and place a slice of cheese on it.
3. Pile the BBQ chicken mixture on top.
4. Add lettuce or coleslaw if you have it.
5. Top with the second slice of bread, press down gently, and enjoy.

Alternatives:

- Grill or toast the sandwich for a warm and crispy version.
- Add pickles or jalapeños for an extra kick.

Quick stir-fries

1. Chicken & Bell Pepper Stir Fry

Serves: 1-2

Ingredients:

- 1/2 cup chicken, diced (leftover or freshly cooked)
- 1/2 cup bell peppers, sliced (any color)
- **Stir Fry Sauce:**
- *Homemade Version:*
  - 2 tablespoons soy sauce
  - 1 tablespoon honey or brown sugar
- *Store-Bought Alternative:* 2 tablespoons of store-bought stir fry sauce

Steps:

1. If making the homemade sauce, mix soy sauce and honey in a small bowl.
2. In a pan over medium heat, cook the chicken until browned.
3. Add the sliced bell peppers and cook until they're tender-crisp.
4. Pour the stir fry sauce (either homemade or store-bought) over the mixture and stir well.
5. Serve hot.

Alternatives:

- Add sliced onions or snap peas for additional flavor and texture.
- Garnish with sesame seeds or chopped green onions.

2. Beef & Broccoli Stir Fry

Serves: 1-2

Ingredients:

- 1/2 cup beef strips
- 1/2 cup broccoli florets
- **Stir Fry Sauce:**
- *Homemade Version:*
    - 2 tablespoons oyster sauce
    - 1 tablespoon water
    - 1 teaspoon cornstarch
- *Store-Bought Alternative:* 2 tablespoons of store-bought beef stir fry sauce

Steps:

1. If using the homemade sauce, mix oyster sauce, water, and cornstarch in a bowl until smooth.
2. In a pan over medium heat, cook the beef strips until nearly done.
3. Add broccoli and continue cooking until it's tender-crisp.
4. Pour the sauce over the beef and broccoli and stir until thickened.
5. Serve immediately.

Alternatives:

- Throw in some thinly sliced carrots or bell peppers for extra crunch.
- Drizzle with a touch of sesame oil for a nutty flavor.

3. Shrimp & Snow Pea Stir Fry

Serves: 1-2

Ingredients:

- 1/2 cup fresh or frozen shrimp, peeled and deveined
- 1/2 cup snow peas, trimmed
- **Stir Fry Sauce:**
- *Homemade Version:*
    - 2 tablespoons soy sauce
    - 1 tablespoon lemon or lime juice
- *Store-Bought Alternative:* 2 tablespoons of store-bought seafood stir fry sauce

Steps:

1. If making the homemade sauce, combine soy sauce and lemon juice in a bowl.
2. In a pan over medium heat, cook the shrimp until they turn pink.
3. Add snow peas and stir fry until bright green and tender.
4. Pour the sauce over the mixture, stir, and serve.

Alternatives:

- Add sliced bell peppers or baby corn for variety.
- Garnish with fresh cilantro or red pepper flakes for added kick.

4. Tofu & Mixed Veggie Stir Fry

Serves: 1-2

Ingredients:

- 1/2 cup firm tofu, diced
- 1/2 cup mixed vegetables (like bell peppers, carrots, and snap peas)
- **Stir Fry Sauce:**
- *Homemade Version:*
    - 2 tablespoons soy sauce
    - 1 tablespoon peanut butter or tahini
    - 1 teaspoon honey or brown sugar
- *Store-Bought Alternative:* 2 tablespoons of store-bought vegetarian stir fry sauce

Steps:

1. For the homemade sauce, whisk together soy sauce, peanut butter, and honey in a bowl until smooth.
2. In a pan over medium heat, fry the tofu cubes until golden.
3. Add mixed vegetables and stir fry until they're vibrant and slightly softened.
4. Pour the sauce over the tofu and veggies, stir until everything is well-coated, and serve.

Alternatives:

- Add cashews or peanuts for a crunchy texture.
- Drizzle with chili oil or add crushed red pepper for a spicy touch.

5. Pork & Green Bean Stir Fry

Serves: 1-2

Ingredients:

- 1/2 cup pork, thinly sliced
- 1/2 cup green beans, trimmed and cut in half
- **Stir Fry Sauce:**
- *Homemade Version:*
    - 2 tablespoons hoisin sauce
    - 1 tablespoon water
- *Store-Bought Alternative:* 2 tablespoons of store-bought pork stir fry sauce

Steps:

1. In a pan over medium heat, cook the pork slices until browned and no longer pink.
2. Add the green beans and stir fry until bright green and tender-crisp.
3. Pour the stir fry sauce (either homemade or store-bought) over the pork and green beans, mix well, and serve.

Alternatives:

- Add thinly sliced bell peppers or onions for extra flavor.
- Top with a sprinkle of sesame seeds or sliced green onions.

Rice Bowls

1. Chicken Teriyaki Rice Bowl

Serves: 1

Ingredients:

- 1/2 cup cooked rice
- 1/2 cup chicken, diced (leftover or freshly cooked)
- **Teriyaki Sauce:**
- *Homemade Version:*
    - 2 tablespoons soy sauce
    - 1 tablespoon brown sugar
    - 1 teaspoon vinegar
- *Store-Bought Alternative:* 2 tablespoons of store-bought teriyaki sauce

Steps:

1. If making the homemade teriyaki sauce, mix soy sauce, brown sugar, and vinegar in a small bowl until sugar dissolves.
2. In a pan over medium heat, cook the chicken. Once it's heated or lightly browned, pour the teriyaki sauce (either homemade or store-bought) over it.
3. Stir until the chicken is well-coated and cooked through.
4. Place the cooked rice in a bowl, then top with the chicken.

Alternatives:

- Add steamed broccoli or bell peppers for extra nutrients.
- Use tofu instead of chicken for a vegetarian version.

2. Veggie & Egg Rice Bowl

Serves: 1

Ingredients:

- 1/2 cup cooked rice
- 1 egg, fried
- 1/2 cup mixed vegetables (like peas, corn, or carrots - frozen mix works well)
- A pinch of salt and pepper

Steps:

1. In a pan over medium heat, cook the mixed vegetables until they're heated through.
2. In the same pan or another, fry the egg to your liking, seasoning it with salt and pepper.
3. Place the cooked rice in a bowl, add the vegetables, and top with the fried egg.

Alternatives:

- Drizzle with soy sauce or a sprinkle of sesame seeds for added flavor.
- Add diced tofu or chicken for extra protein.

3. Spicy Chicken Rice Bowl

Serves: 1

Ingredients:

- 1/2 cup cooked rice
- 1/2 cup chicken, diced (leftover or freshly cooked)
- **Spicy Sauce:**
- *Homemade Version:*
  - 2 tablespoons soy sauce
  - 1 tablespoon sriracha or hot sauce
- *Store-Bought Alternative:* 2 tablespoons of store-bought spicy Asian sauce

Steps:

1. If making the homemade spicy sauce, mix soy sauce and sriracha in a small bowl.
2. In a pan over medium heat, cook the chicken. Once it's heated or lightly browned, pour the spicy sauce (either homemade or store-bought) over it.
3. Stir until the chicken is well-coated and cooked through.
4. Place the cooked rice in a bowl, then top with the spicy chicken.

Alternatives:

- Add sautéed bell peppers or onions for extra flavor.
- Sprinkle with green onions or sesame seeds for added texture.

4. Sweet & Sour Tofu Rice Bowl

Serves: 1

Ingredients:

- 1/2 cup cooked rice
- 1/2 cup tofu, diced
- **Sweet & Sour Sauce:**
- *Homemade Version:*
    - 2 tablespoons ketchup
    - 1 tablespoon vinegar
    - 1 tablespoon brown sugar
- *Store-Bought Alternative:* 2 tablespoons of store-bought sweet & sour sauce

Steps:

1. If making the homemade sauce, combine ketchup, vinegar, and brown sugar in a bowl, stirring until well mixed.
2. In a pan over medium heat, fry the tofu cubes until golden.
3. Pour the sweet & sour sauce (either homemade or store-bought) over the tofu.
4. Stir until the tofu is well-coated.
5. Serve the tofu over the cooked rice.

Alternatives:

- Add pineapple chunks or bell pepper strips for a more traditional touch.
- Replace tofu with chicken or shrimp, if desired.

5. Beef & Broccoli Rice Bowl

Serves: 1

Ingredients:

- 1/2 cup cooked rice
- 1/2 cup beef strips
- 1/2 cup broccoli florets
- **Beef Sauce:**
- *Homemade Version:*
    - 2 tablespoons soy sauce
    - 1 tablespoon brown sugar
    - 1 teaspoon cornstarch dissolved in 1 tablespoon water
- *Store-Bought Alternative:* 2 tablespoons of store-bought beef stir-fry sauce

Steps:

1. If making the homemade sauce, mix soy sauce, brown sugar, and the cornstarch-water mixture in a bowl.
2. In a pan over medium heat, cook the beef strips until nearly done. Add broccoli and continue to cook until it's tender-crisp.
3. Pour the beef sauce (either homemade or store-bought) over the beef and broccoli.
4. Stir and cook until the sauce thickens and coats everything.
5. Serve the beef and broccoli over the rice.

Alternatives:

- Add thinly sliced bell peppers or snap peas for extra crunch.
- Sprinkle it with toasted sesame seeds or sliced green onions for garnish.

DIY Instant Noodles in a Jar

1. Spicy Chicken Instant Noodles in a Jar

Serves: 1

Ingredients:

- 1 serving instant noodles (discard flavor packet or keep for a later use)
- 1 teaspoon chicken bouillon powder or a small cube
- 1/4 cup cooked chicken, shredded (leftovers work perfectly)
- 1/4 cup frozen mixed vegetables (like peas, corn, and carrot bits)
- 1/2 teaspoon chili flakes (adjust based on heat preference)
- A slice of lime (optional)
- Boiling water

Steps:

1. In a clean jar, layer the uncooked noodles at the bottom.
2. Add the chicken bouillon powder or cube over the noodles.
3. Layer in the shredded chicken, followed by the frozen mixed vegetables.
4. Sprinkle chili flakes on top.
5. When ready to eat, pour boiling water into the jar, ensuring all ingredients are submerged. Seal the jar and let sit for about 3-4 minutes.
6. Stir well, squeeze in the lime slice if using, and enjoy straight from the jar!

Alternatives:

- Swap chicken with tofu cubes for a vegetarian twist.
- Add a dollop of peanut butter for a creamy and nutty flavor.

2. Miso Veggie Instant Noodles in a Jar

Serves: 1

Ingredients:

- 1 serving instant noodles (discard flavor packet or keep for a later use)
- 1 tablespoon miso paste
- 1/4 cup fresh or frozen spinach
- 1/4 cup sliced mushrooms (like shiitake or button)
- 1 green onion, sliced
- 1/2 teaspoon sesame seeds (optional)
- Boiling water

Steps:

1. In a jar, place the uncooked noodles at the base.
2. Layer in the miso paste, spreading it a bit with a spoon.
3. Add the spinach and mushrooms over the miso.
4. Top with sliced green onion and sprinkle sesame seeds if using.
5. When you're hungry, pour boiling water into the jar, submerging all the components. Close the lid and let it sit for 3-4 minutes.
6. Stir thoroughly, ensuring the miso is dissolved into the broth, and savor your meal from the jar!

Alternatives:

- Add tofu or edamame beans for an added protein punch.
- Include a dash of chili oil or sriracha for some spice.

Chapter 4

Simple Dinners

One-pot pasta dishes

These One-pot pasta dishes are crafted to serve two, making it perfect for sharing a meal with a flatmate or friend. After all, food tastes better when enjoyed together, right? Plus, it's a smart way to split the grocery bill!

But what if it's just you? No worries! The other serving can be a lifesaver for those ultra-busy days.

Storing Leftovers:

- Cooling: Before storing, let your dish come to room temperature. This usually takes about 20-30 minutes. This is important to prevent bacteria growth.
- Storing: Transfer your cooled pasta dish to an airtight container. This will help retain its freshness.
- Refrigerating: Your one-pot pasta can be stored in the fridge for up to 3 days.

Reheating Your Dish:

Pasta can get a bit tricky when reheating, especially if it's a creamy or cheesy dish. But with a couple of tweaks, you can enjoy your meal just like it was freshly made!

- Microwave: Transfer your pasta to a microwave-safe dish. If your pasta looks a bit dry, sprinkle some water or broth over it to keep it moist. Cover with a microwave-safe lid or plastic wrap, leaving a small corner open for steam to escape. Heat in 1-minute intervals, stirring in between, until hot.
- Stovetop: Pour your pasta into a pan. If needed, add a little water, broth, or milk to bring back its creaminess. Warm it over medium heat, stirring occasionally, until heated through.

1. Garlic Parmesan Spaghetti

Serves: 2

Ingredients:

- 200g spaghetti
- 2 tablespoons olive oil
- 4 garlic cloves, minced
- 2 cups chicken or vegetable broth
- 1 cup water
- 1/2 cup grated Parmesan cheese
- Salt and pepper to taste
- Fresh parsley, chopped (optional for garnish)

Steps:

1. In a large pot, heat olive oil over medium heat. Add the minced garlic and sauté until fragrant.
2. Add the spaghetti, broth, and water. Season with salt and pepper.
3. Increase the heat to high and bring the mixture to a boil. Once boiling, reduce the heat to medium and simmer until the pasta is cooked through and the liquid has reduced, about 10-12 minutes.
4. Remove from heat and stir in the Parmesan cheese until well combined.
5. Serve hot and garnish with parsley if available.

Alternatives:

- Add chili flakes for a spicy kick.
- Toss in some frozen peas or diced bell pepper for added veggies.

2. Creamy Tomato and Basil Pasta

Serves: 2

Ingredients:

- 200g penne pasta
- 1 can (400g) diced tomatoes
- 2 cups vegetable broth or water
- 1/2 cup cream or milk
- 1/4 cup fresh basil, chopped (or 1 tablespoon dried basil)
- 1 tablespoon olive oil
- Salt and pepper to taste

Steps:

1. In a pot, heat olive oil over medium heat. Add the diced tomatoes and cook for a few minutes.
2. Add the pasta, vegetable broth (or water), and dried basil (if using fresh basil, add it later).
3. Bring the mixture to a boil, then reduce the heat and simmer until the pasta is cooked, about 10-12 minutes.
4. Once the pasta is done, stir in the cream or milk and fresh basil if you have it. Season with salt and pepper.
5. Serve immediately.

Alternatives:

- Add some grated cheese on top for a cheesy finish.
- Toss in cooked chicken or sausage pieces for added protein.

3. One-Pot Pesto Pasta

Serves: 2

Ingredients:

- 200g fusilli or any spiral pasta
- 2 cups chicken or vegetable broth
- 3 tablespoons store-bought pesto
- 1 tablespoon olive oil
- 1/4 cup grated Parmesan cheese
- Salt to taste

Steps:

1. In a pot, heat olive oil over medium heat. Add the pasta and broth.
2. Bring to a boil, then reduce the heat to a simmer. Cook until the pasta is tender and most of the broth is absorbed, about 10-12 minutes.
3. Stir in the pesto and Parmesan cheese, mixing until the pasta is well coated.
4. Season with salt and serve.

Alternatives:

- Add cherry tomatoes or spinach for added freshness.
- Incorporate cooked shrimp or diced chicken for a protein-packed dish.

4. One-Pot Chili Mac

Serves: 2

Ingredients:

- 200g elbow macaroni
- 1 can (400g) kidney beans, drained and rinsed
- 1 can (400g) diced tomatoes
- 2 cups vegetable or beef broth
- 1 tablespoon chili powder
- 1/2 cup grated cheddar cheese
- Salt and pepper to taste

Steps:

1. In a pot over medium heat, combine macaroni, beans, tomatoes, broth, and chili powder.
2. Bring the mixture to a boil, then reduce to a simmer. Cook until pasta is tender, about 10-12 minutes.
3. Stir in the cheddar cheese until melted and creamy.
4. Season with salt and pepper. Serve hot.

Alternatives:

- Add diced bell peppers or corn for extra veggies.
- Stir in some ground beef or turkey for a meatier version.

5. One-Pot Lemon Garlic Pasta

Serves: 2

Ingredients:

- 200g spaghetti or linguine
- 2 cups vegetable or chicken broth
- 4 garlic cloves, minced
- 1 lemon, zest and juice
- 2 tablespoons olive oil
- Fresh parsley, chopped (optional for garnish)
- Salt to taste

Steps:

1. In a pot, heat olive oil over medium heat. Add the minced garlic and sauté briefly.
2. Add pasta, broth, lemon zest, and lemon juice.
3. Bring to a boil, then reduce to a simmer. Cook until pasta is al dente, about 10-12 minutes.
4. Season with salt. Garnish with parsley if available. Serve immediately.

Alternatives:

- Top with grated Parmesan cheese.
- Add chili flakes for a touch of heat.

6. One-Pot Creamy Mushroom Pasta

Serves: 2

Ingredients:

- 200g fettuccine or penne
- 1 cup mushrooms, sliced
- 2 cups vegetable or chicken broth
- 1/2 cup cream or milk
- 1 tablespoon olive oil
- Salt and pepper to taste

Steps:

1. In a pot, heat olive oil. Add sliced mushrooms and sauté until browned.
2. Add pasta and broth to the pot.
3. Bring to a boil, then reduce heat to simmer. Cook until pasta is almost done, about 8-10 minutes.
4. Stir in the cream or milk and continue cooking until pasta is fully cooked and sauce is creamy.
5. Season with salt and pepper. Serve hot.

Alternatives:

- Add spinach or peas for a green touch.
- Stir in cooked chicken or bacon bits for added protein.

7. One-Pot Taco Pasta

Serves: 2

Ingredients:

- 200g shell pasta or rotini
- 1 cup canned black beans, drained and rinsed
- 1 can (400g) diced tomatoes
- 2 cups beef or vegetable broth
- 1 tablespoon taco seasoning
- 1/2 cup grated cheddar cheese
- Salt to taste

Steps:

1. In a pot, combine pasta, black beans, tomatoes, broth, and taco seasoning.
2. Bring the mixture to a boil, then simmer until pasta is tender, about 10-12 minutes.
3. Stir in the cheddar cheese until creamy.
4. Season with salt. Serve immediately.

Alternatives:

- Top with sour cream or avocado slices.
- Add ground beef or turkey for a meatier dish.

8. One-Pot Broccoli Alfredo Pasta

Serves: 2

Ingredients:

- 200g fettuccine or linguine
- 1 cup broccoli florets
- 2 cups vegetable or chicken broth
- 1/2 cup cream or milk
- 1/2 cup grated Parmesan cheese
- 1 tablespoon olive oil
- Salt and pepper to taste

Steps:

1. In a pot, heat olive oil over medium heat. Add broccoli florets and sauté until slightly tender.
2. Add pasta and broth.
3. Bring the mixture to a boil, then reduce to a simmer. Cook until the pasta is almost done, about 8-10 minutes.
4. Stir in the cream and Parmesan cheese, continuing to cook until the pasta is al dente and the sauce thickens.
5. Season with salt and pepper. Serve immediately.

Alternatives:

- Stir in minced garlic with the broccoli for added flavor.
- Substitute broccoli with cauliflower or asparagus

9. One-Pot Cajun Spice Pasta

Serves: 2

Ingredients:

- 200g penne or rotini
- 1 bell pepper, thinly sliced
- 1 small onion, thinly sliced
- 2 cups vegetable or chicken broth
- 2 tablespoons Cajun spice mix
- 1/2 cup cream or milk
- 1 tablespoon olive oil
- Salt to taste

Steps:

1. In a pot, heat olive oil. Add bell pepper and onion slices, sautéing until they start to soften.
2. Add the pasta, Cajun spice mix, and broth.
3. Bring to a boil, then reduce to a simmer. Let it cook until pasta is nearly done, about 8-10 minutes.
4. Pour in the cream, stirring occasionally until the pasta is cooked and the sauce thickens.
5. Season with salt. Serve hot.

Alternatives:

- Add cooked shrimp or chicken pieces for added protein.
- Sprinkle with grated cheese before serving.

10. One-Pot Sun-dried Tomato and Spinach Pasta

Serves: 2

Ingredients:

- 200g spaghetti or linguine
- 1/2 cup sun-dried tomatoes, chopped
- 1 cup fresh spinach
- 2 cups vegetable or chicken broth
- 1/2 cup grated Parmesan cheese
- 1 tablespoon olive oil
- 2 garlic cloves, minced
- Salt and pepper to taste

Steps:

1. In a pot, heat olive oil over medium heat. Add minced garlic and sun-dried tomatoes, sautéing for a couple of minutes.
2. Pour in the broth and add pasta.
3. Bring to a boil, then simmer. Cook until the pasta is almost done, around 8-10 minutes.
4. Add spinach, stirring until it wilts. Sprinkle in the Parmesan cheese, stirring until creamy.
5. Season with salt and pepper. Serve immediately.

Alternatives:

- Use kale or arugula instead of spinach.
- Incorporate chili flakes for a bit of heat.

11. One-Pot Greek Pasta

Serves: 2

Ingredients:

- 200g penne pasta
- 1 cup cherry tomatoes, halved
- 1/4 cup black olives, sliced
- 1/4 cup feta cheese, crumbled
- 2 cups vegetable or chicken broth
- 1 tablespoon olive oil
- 2 garlic cloves, minced
- Salt and pepper to taste

Steps:

1. In a pot, heat olive oil over medium heat. Add minced garlic and sauté for a minute.
2. Add the pasta and broth.
3. Bring to a boil, then reduce to a simmer, cooking until the pasta is almost done, about 8-10 minutes.
4. Stir in the cherry tomatoes, olives, and feta cheese.
5. Cook for an additional 2-3 minutes until everything is heated through.
6. Season with salt and pepper. Serve immediately.

Alternatives:

- Add diced cucumber for a refreshing touch.
- Sprinkle with dried oregano for added flavor.

12. One-Pot Pesto and Pea Pasta

Serves: 2

Ingredients:

- 200g fusilli or spaghetti
- 1/2 cup green peas (fresh or frozen)
- 3 tablespoons store-bought pesto sauce
- 2 cups vegetable or chicken broth
- 1/2 cup grated Parmesan cheese
- Salt to taste

Steps:

1. In a pot over medium heat, combine pasta, peas, and broth.
2. Bring the mixture to a boil, then simmer until the pasta is al dente, about 8-10 minutes.
3. Stir in the pesto sauce and Parmesan cheese until well combined.
4. Season with salt. Serve hot.

Alternatives:

- Add diced bell pepper for added color and flavor.
- Stir in some pine nuts or sliced almonds for a crunchy texture.

13. One-Pot Tomato Basil Pasta

Serves: 2

Ingredients:

- 200g spaghetti
- 1 can (400g) diced tomatoes
- 2 cups vegetable or chicken broth
- 1/4 cup fresh basil, chopped (or 1 tablespoon dried basil)
- 1 tablespoon olive oil
- 2 garlic cloves, minced
- Salt and pepper to taste

Steps:

1. In a pot, heat olive oil over medium heat. Add minced garlic and sauté until fragrant.
2. Add the pasta, diced tomatoes, and broth.
3. Bring to a boil, then reduce to a simmer, letting it cook until the pasta is nearly done, about 8-10 minutes.
4. Stir in the fresh or dried basil and cook for another 2 minutes.
5. Season with salt and pepper. Serve immediately.

Alternatives:

- Top with some grated mozzarella or cheddar cheese.
- Add red chili flakes for a spicy kick.

Sheet Pan Meals

1. Lemon Herb Chicken & Potatoes

Serves: 2

Ingredients:

- 2 chicken breasts
- 2 medium potatoes, diced
- 2 tablespoons olive oil
- 1 lemon, zest and juice
- 1 teaspoon dried oregano
- Salt and pepper to taste

Steps:

1. Preheat the oven to 200°C (400°F).
2. In a bowl, combine olive oil, lemon zest, lemon juice, oregano, salt, and pepper.
3. Toss the chicken breasts and diced potatoes in the mixture until well coated.
4. Spread them out on a baking sheet.
5. Roast in the oven for 25-30 minutes, or until the chicken is cooked through and the potatoes are golden.
6. Serve immediately.

Alternatives:

- Swap potatoes for sweet potatoes or baby carrots for a different root vegetable experience.
- For a spicy kick, add a pinch of chili flakes or cayenne pepper to the marinade.

2. Spiced Chickpea & Veggie Tray

Serves: 2

Ingredients:

- 1 can chickpeas, drained and rinsed
- 1 bell pepper, sliced
- 1 zucchini, sliced
- 2 tablespoons olive oil
- 1 teaspoon smoked paprika
- 1/2 teaspoon cumin
- Salt and pepper to taste

Steps:

1. Preheat the oven to 200°C (400°F).
2. In a bowl, mix olive oil, smoked paprika, cumin, salt, and pepper.
3. Add chickpeas, bell pepper, and zucchini to the bowl and toss until well coated.
4. Spread the mixture on a baking sheet.
5. Roast for 20-25 minutes, or until the veggies are tender and chickpeas are slightly crispy.
6. Serve immediately.

Alternatives:

- Replace the zucchini with eggplant slices or mushrooms.
- For added protein, sprinkle some feta cheese on top before serving.

3. Honey Mustard Salmon & Asparagus

Serves: 2

Ingredients:

- 2 salmon fillets
- 1 bunch of asparagus, trimmed
- 2 tablespoons honey
- 2 tablespoons Dijon mustard
- 1 tablespoon olive oil
- Salt and pepper to taste

Steps:

1. Preheat the oven to 200°C (400°F).
2. In a bowl, mix honey, Dijon mustard, olive oil, salt, and pepper.
3. Coat the salmon fillets and asparagus with the honey mustard mixture.
4. Place them on a baking sheet.
5. Roast for 15-20 minutes, or until the salmon flakes easily with a fork.
6. Serve immediately.

Alternatives:

- Swap asparagus for green beans or tenderstem broccoli.
- If you're not a fan of honey mustard, use maple syrup or agave nectar in place of honey for a different sweet touch.

4. Teriyaki Tofu & Broccoli

Serves: 2

Ingredients:

- 1 block of firm tofu, cubed
- 1 head of broccoli, cut into florets
- 1/4 cup teriyaki sauce (store-bought)
- 1 tablespoon olive oil
- 1 tablespoon sesame seeds (optional)

Steps:

1. Preheat the oven to 200°C (400°F).
2. In a bowl, toss tofu cubes and broccoli florets with olive oil and teriyaki sauce.
3. Spread them out on a baking sheet.
4. Roast for 20-25 minutes, or until tofu is golden and broccoli is tender.
5. Sprinkle with sesame seeds if desired. Serve immediately.

Alternatives:

- If broccoli isn't your thing, try snap peas or bell peppers instead.
- For a spicy teriyaki twist, add some sriracha or chili paste to the teriyaki sauce before tossing.

5. BBQ Sausage & Mixed Veggies

Serves: 2

Ingredients:

- 4 sausages of your choice
- 1 bell pepper, sliced
- 1 red onion, sliced
- 1 cup cherry tomatoes
- 2 tablespoons BBQ sauce
- 1 tablespoon olive oil

Steps:

1. Preheat the oven to 200°C (400°F).
2. In a bowl, combine the veggies, sausages, BBQ sauce, and olive oil.
3. Spread the mixture on a baking sheet.
4. Roast for 25-30 minutes, turning the sausages halfway, until they're cooked through and the veggies are tender.
5. Serve immediately.

Alternatives:

- Swap out regular sausages for plant-based/vegetarian sausages for a meatless version.
- Try different BBQ sauce flavors, like honey BBQ or spicy BBQ, to change up the taste.

6. Garlic Parmesan Shrimp & Green Beans

Serves: 2

Ingredients:

- 200g shrimp, peeled and deveined
- 200g green beans, trimmed
- 3 garlic cloves, minced
- 2 tablespoons olive oil
- 1/4 cup grated Parmesan cheese
- Salt and pepper to taste

Steps:

1. Preheat the oven to 200°C (400°F).
2. In a bowl, mix olive oil, minced garlic, salt, and pepper.
3. Add shrimp and green beans, tossing until well coated.
4. Spread them on a baking sheet and sprinkle with Parmesan cheese.
5. Roast for 10-15 minutes, or until shrimp turn pink.
6. Serve immediately.

Alternatives:

- Use snow peas or asparagus in place of green beans.
- Add lemon zest to the olive oil mixture for a refreshing citrus note.

7. Balsamic Chicken & Root Veggies

Serves: 2

Ingredients:

- 2 chicken thighs or breasts
- 1 carrot, sliced
- 1 parsnip, sliced
- 2 small potatoes, diced
- 3 tablespoons balsamic vinegar
- 2 tablespoons olive oil
- Salt and pepper to taste

Steps:

1. Preheat the oven to 200°C (400°F).
2. Mix balsamic vinegar, olive oil, salt, and pepper in a bowl.
3. Toss chicken and veggies in the mixture.
4. Spread evenly on a baking sheet.
5. Roast for 30-35 minutes, or until chicken is cooked through and veggies are tender.
6. Serve immediately.

Alternatives:

- Substitute sweet potatoes for regular potatoes.
- Add a sprinkle of feta cheese on top before serving.

8. Spicy Sausage & Bell Peppers

Serves: 2

Ingredients:

- 4 spicy sausages (like chorizo or Italian spicy sausage)
- 2 bell peppers, sliced
- 1 red onion, sliced
- 2 tablespoons olive oil
- 1 teaspoon chili flakes (optional)
- Salt to taste

Steps:

1. Preheat the oven to 200°C (400°F).
2. In a bowl, toss bell peppers, onion, olive oil, chili flakes, and salt.
3. Place sausages and veggies on a baking sheet.
4. Roast for 25-30 minutes, turning sausages halfway, until they're browned and veggies are caramelized.
5. Serve hot.

Alternatives:

- Use chicken sausages for a leaner option.
- Add cherry tomatoes for a juicy burst.

9. Rosemary Lemon Tilapia & Zucchini

Serves: 2

Ingredients:

- 2 tilapia fillets
- 2 zucchinis, sliced
- 2 tablespoons olive oil
- 1 lemon, zest and juice
- 1 teaspoon dried rosemary
- Salt and pepper to taste

Steps:

1. Preheat the oven to 200°C (400°F).
2. In a bowl, mix olive oil, lemon zest, lemon juice, rosemary, salt, and pepper.
3. Coat tilapia and zucchini slices in the mixture.
4. Spread on a baking sheet.
5. Roast for 20-25 minutes, or until the fish is flaky.
6. Serve immediately.

Alternatives:

- Replace zucchini with green beans or asparagus.
- Use lime instead of lemon for a different citrus note.

10. Cumin Roasted Chickpea & Sweet Potato

Serves: 2

Ingredients:

- 1 can chickpeas, drained and rinsed
- 2 sweet potatoes, diced
- 2 tablespoons olive oil
- 2 teaspoons ground cumin
- Salt and pepper to taste

Steps:

1. Preheat the oven to 200°C (400°F).
2. Toss chickpeas and sweet potatoes with olive oil, cumin, salt, and pepper.
3. Spread on a baking sheet.
4. Roast for 25-30 minutes, stirring halfway, until sweet potatoes are tender and chickpeas are slightly crispy.
5. Serve hot.

Alternatives:

- Sprinkle with some feta or goat cheese before serving.
- Add some bell peppers for color and extra flavor.

11. BBQ Tempeh & Broccoli

Serves: 2

Ingredients:

- 200g tempeh, sliced
- 1 head of broccoli, cut into florets
- 3 tablespoons BBQ sauce
- 2 tablespoons olive oil

Steps:

1. Preheat the oven to 200°C (400°F).
2. In a bowl, toss tempeh slices and broccoli with BBQ sauce and olive oil.
3. Spread on a baking sheet.
4. Roast for 20-25 minutes, or until tempeh is browned and broccoli is crispy at the edges.
5. Serve immediately.

Alternatives:

- Add sliced bell peppers or carrots for more veggies.
- Drizzle with some hot sauce for extra kick.

12. Greek Lemon Oregano Tofu & Tomatoes

Serves: 2

Ingredients:

- 200g firm tofu, cubed
- 2 cups cherry tomatoes
- 2 tablespoons olive oil
- Zest and juice of 1 lemon
- 1 teaspoon dried oregano
- Salt to taste

Steps:

1. Preheat the oven to 200°C (400°F).
2. In a bowl, toss tofu cubes and cherry tomatoes with olive oil, lemon zest, lemon juice, oregano, and salt.
3. Spread on a baking sheet.
4. Roast for 20-25 minutes, or until tofu is golden and tomatoes are blistered.
5. Serve hot.

Alternatives:

- Sprinkle with crumbled feta cheese.
- Add some olives for a briny touch.

Quick Curries

Spice Up Your Meals

Embark on a culinary journey with these quick curry dishes, each tailored to serve two. Perfect for sharing with a roommate, or perhaps during a casual date night in. After all, nothing beats the joy of sharing a flavorsome homemade curry with someone! And hey, pairing up for cooking is a clever way to split the grocery costs.

But if you're dining alone tonight, that's alright! That extra serving comes in handy for those unexpected late nights or when you simply can't muster up the energy to cook from scratch.

Storing Leftovers:

- Cooling: Before stashing it away, ensure your curry cools down to room temperature, usually around 20-30 minutes. It's a crucial step to keep those pesky bacteria at bay.
- Storing: Once cooled, shift your curry to an airtight container to maintain its freshness.
- Refrigerating: Your delicious curry is good in the fridge for up to 3 days.

Reheating Your Dish:

Curry, unlike some other dishes, often becomes even more flavorful the next day. When reheating:

- Microwave: Pour the desired amount into a microwave-safe bowl. Use a microwave-safe lid or plastic wrap to cover, ensuring a small corner is open for steam. Warm it up in 1-minute bursts, stirring

between each to ensure even heating.
- Stovetop: Move your curry to a pan. Gently reheat it on medium, stirring occasionally, until it's piping hot and ready to be devoured again.

1. Chickpea Coconut Curry

Serves: 2

Ingredients:

- 1 can chickpeas, drained and rinsed
- 1 can (400ml) coconut milk
- 2 tablespoons curry powder
- 1 onion, diced
- 2 garlic cloves, minced
- 2 tablespoons vegetable oil
- Salt to taste

Steps:

1. In a pan, heat the vegetable oil over medium heat. Add onions and sauté until translucent.
2. Add garlic and sauté for another minute.
3. Stir in the curry powder until the onions and garlic are coated.
4. Pour in the coconut milk and chickpeas. Stir well.
5. Let it simmer for 10-15 minutes until it thickens slightly.
6. Season with salt and serve over rice.

Alternatives:

- Add spinach or kale for some greens.
- Swap chickpeas for boiled potatoes or tofu cubes.

2. Quick Chicken Curry

Serves: 2

Ingredients:

- 2 chicken breasts, diced
- 1 can (400ml) diced tomatoes
- 2 tablespoons curry paste (like Tikka Masala or Madras)
- 1 onion, chopped
- 1 tablespoon vegetable oil
- Salt and pepper to taste

Steps:

1. Heat oil in a pan and sauté the onion until golden.
2. Add the chicken pieces and brown them slightly.
3. Stir in the curry paste, ensuring chicken pieces are well coated.
4. Pour in the diced tomatoes, mixing well.
5. Let it simmer for 15-20 minutes until the chicken is cooked through.
6. Season with salt and pepper. Serve with rice or naan bread.

Alternatives:

- Add bell peppers or peas for more veggies.
- Use pre-cooked or leftover chicken to reduce cooking time.

3. Simple Veggie Curry

Serves: 2

Ingredients:

- 2 cups mixed veggies (like bell peppers, zucchini, and carrots), chopped
- 1 can (400ml) coconut milk
- 2 tablespoons curry powder or paste
- 1 onion, diced
- 2 garlic cloves, minced
- 1 tablespoon vegetable oil
- Salt to taste

Steps:

1. In a pan, heat the oil and sauté the onions and garlic.
2. Add the veggies and cook for a few minutes until they begin to soften.
3. Stir in the curry powder or paste.
4. Pour in the coconut milk, mixing well.
5. Let it simmer for 10-15 minutes. Season with salt.
6. Serve with rice or bread.

Alternatives:

- Add chickpeas or tofu for added protein.
- Garnish with fresh cilantro for a fresh touch.

4. Quick Beef Curry

Serves: 2

Ingredients:

- 300g beef chunks or ground beef
- 1 can (400ml) diced tomatoes
- 1 onion, chopped
- 2 teaspoons curry powder
- 1 tablespoon vegetable oil
- Salt and pepper to taste

Steps:

1. In a pan, heat oil and sauté the onion until golden.
2. Add beef and brown it.
3. Stir in curry powder.
4. Pour in the diced tomatoes and mix well.
5. Cover and let it simmer for 20-25 minutes, stirring occasionally.
6. Season with salt and pepper, serve with rice.

Alternatives:

- Add green peas or cubed potatoes for variety.
- Garnish with fresh parsley or cilantro.

5. Lamb Keema Curry

Serves: 2

Ingredients:

- 300g ground lamb
- 1 can (400ml) diced tomatoes
- 1 onion, chopped
- 2 teaspoons garam masala
- 1 tablespoon vegetable oil
- Salt to taste

Steps:

1. Heat oil in a pan, add onions, and sauté until soft.
2. Add ground lamb and cook until browned.
3. Sprinkle in garam masala and stir.
4. Add diced tomatoes, mix, and let it simmer for 15-20 minutes.
5. Season with salt and serve with naan or rice.

Alternatives:

- Add bell peppers or green peas for added texture.
- Spice it up with a pinch of chili powder.

6. Turkey & Spinach Curry

Serves: 2

Ingredients:

- 300g ground turkey
- 3 cups spinach, chopped
- 1 can (400ml) coconut milk
- 1 onion, chopped
- 2 teaspoons curry paste (like Tikka Masala or Madras)
- 1 tablespoon vegetable oil
- Salt to taste

Steps:

1. In a pan, heat oil and sauté the onion until translucent.
2. Add ground turkey and cook until browned.
3. Stir in curry paste.
4. Add chopped spinach and stir until wilted.
5. Pour in coconut milk, let it simmer for 15-20 minutes.
6. Season with salt and serve with rice.

Alternatives:

- Replace spinach with kale or Swiss chard.
- Use ground chicken in place of turkey.

7. Pork & Apple Curry

Serves: 2

Ingredients:

- 300g diced pork
- 1 apple, peeled and diced
- 1 onion, chopped
- 1 can (400ml) diced tomatoes
- 2 teaspoons curry powder
- 1 tablespoon vegetable oil
- Salt and pepper to taste

Steps:

1. Heat oil in a pan and sauté onion until golden.
2. Add pork chunks and brown them.
3. Stir in the curry powder.
4. Add the diced apple and tomatoes. Mix well.
5. Let it simmer for 20-25 minutes until pork is cooked through.
6. Season with salt and pepper, serve with bread or rice.

Alternatives:

- Add a touch of cinnamon or nutmeg for added warmth.
- Swap apple with pear for a different fruity twist.

8. Chicken & Bell Pepper Curry

Serves: 2

Ingredients:

- 2 chicken breasts, diced
- 1 bell pepper, sliced
- 1 onion, chopped
- 1 can (400ml) coconut milk
- 2 teaspoons curry paste (e.g., green curry paste)
- 1 tablespoon vegetable oil
- Salt to taste

Steps:

1. Heat oil in a pan and sauté onion until soft.
2. Add diced chicken and cook until slightly browned.
3. Stir in curry paste.
4. Add bell pepper slices, stir for a minute.
5. Pour in coconut milk and let it simmer for 15-20 minutes.
6. Season with salt and serve with rice.

Alternatives:

- Add bamboo shoots or baby corn for variety.
- Garnish with fresh basil leaves or lime zest.

9. Creamy Tomato Chicken Curry

Serves: 2

Ingredients:

- 2 chicken breasts, diced
- 1 can (400ml) diced tomatoes
- 1/4 cup cream or yogurt
- 1 onion, chopped
- 2 teaspoons curry powder
- 1 tablespoon vegetable oil
- Salt to taste

Steps:

1. In a pan, heat oil and sauté the onion until golden.
2. Add chicken pieces and brown them.
3. Stir in curry powder.
4. Pour in the diced tomatoes and mix well.
5. Let it simmer for 20 minutes.
6. Stir in cream or yogurt, season with salt, and simmer for another 5 minutes.
7. Serve with rice or bread.

Alternatives:

- Add fresh cilantro for garnish.
- Introduce bell peppers or peas for added veggies.

10. Spicy Beef & Potato Curry

Serves: 2

Ingredients:

- 300g beef chunks
- 2 medium potatoes, diced
- 1 can (400ml) coconut milk
- 1 onion, chopped
- 2 teaspoons red curry paste
- 1 tablespoon vegetable oil
- Salt and pepper to taste

Steps:

- Heat oil in a pan and sauté onion until translucent.
- Add beef chunks and brown them.
- Stir in red curry paste.
- Introduce diced potatoes and mix well.
- Pour in coconut milk and bring to a simmer.
- Let it cook for 25-30 minutes or until beef and potatoes are tender.
- Season with salt and pepper, then serve with rice.

Alternatives:

- Add green beans or carrots for added nutrition.
- Use green curry paste for a milder flavor.

11. Pork Vindaloo Curry

Serves: 2

Ingredients:

- 300g diced pork
- 1 can (400ml) diced tomatoes
- 1 onion, chopped
- 2 garlic cloves, minced
- 1 tablespoon vindaloo curry paste
- 1 tablespoon vegetable oil
- Salt to taste

Steps:

1. In a pan, heat oil and sauté the onion and garlic until golden.
2. Add diced pork and brown it.
3. Stir in vindaloo curry paste.
4. Pour in the diced tomatoes, mix well, and cover.
5. Let it simmer for 20-25 minutes, until pork is cooked through.
6. Season with salt and serve with rice or naan.

Alternatives:

- Toss in cubed potatoes for a hearty touch.
- Garnish with fresh cilantro.

12. Lamb & Apricot Curry

Serves: 2

Ingredients:

- 300g lamb chunks
- 1/4 cup dried apricots, diced
- 1 can (400ml) coconut milk
- 1 onion, chopped
- 2 teaspoons curry powder
- 1 tablespoon vegetable oil
- Salt and pepper to taste

Steps:

1. Heat oil in a pan and sauté onion until soft.
2. Add lamb chunks and brown them.
3. Stir in curry powder.
4. Add dried apricots and coconut milk, mixing thoroughly.
5. Cover and simmer for 25-30 minutes, or until lamb is tender.
6. Season with salt and pepper, then serve with rice.

Alternatives:

- Use prunes or raisins instead of apricots.
- Garnish with slivered almonds for a crunch.

Tacos & fajitas

1. *Classic Beef Tacos*

Serves: 2

Ingredients:

- 300g ground beef
- 1 packet taco seasoning
- 4 small tortillas
- 1 tomato, diced
- 1 cup lettuce, shredded
- 1/2 cup shredded cheddar cheese

Steps:

1. Cook ground beef in a pan over medium heat until browned.
2. Stir in taco seasoning and follow packet instructions.
3. Assemble tacos by layering beef, lettuce, tomato, and cheese on tortillas.

Alternatives:

- Use ground turkey for a leaner option.
- Add a dollop of sour cream or guacamole.

2. Chicken Fajitas

Serves: 2

Ingredients:

- 2 chicken breasts, sliced
- 1 bell pepper, sliced
- 1 onion, sliced
- 1 packet fajita seasoning
- 4 small tortillas

Steps:

1. Cook chicken in a pan over medium heat until cooked through.
2. Add bell pepper and onion, sauté until soft.
3. Stir in fajita seasoning and follow packet instructions.
4. Serve on tortillas.

Alternatives:

- Add a splash of lime juice for tang.
- Top with a sprinkle of shredded cheese.

3. Veggie Tacos

Serves: 2

Ingredients:

- 1 can black beans, drained and rinsed
- 1 cup corn kernels
- 1 avocado, sliced
- 1 cup lettuce, shredded
- 4 small tortillas

Steps:

1. Heat black beans and corn in a pan until warm.
2. Assemble tacos by layering beans, corn, lettuce, and avocado on tortillas.

Alternatives:

- Use pinto beans instead of black beans.
- Add diced tomatoes for extra flavor.

4. Shrimp Fajitas

Serves: 2

Ingredients:

- 200g shrimp, peeled and deveined
- 1 bell pepper, sliced
- 1 onion, sliced
- 1 packet fajita seasoning
- 4 small tortillas

Steps:

1. Cook shrimp in a pan over medium heat until pink.
2. Add bell pepper and onion, sauté until soft.
3. Stir in fajita seasoning and follow packet instructions.
4. Serve on tortillas.

Alternatives:

- Use chicken or beef strips as an alternative to shrimp.
- Add a squeeze of lemon for extra zing.

5. Spicy Pork Tacos

Serves: 2

Ingredients:

- 300g diced pork
- 1 packet taco seasoning
- 1 jalapeño, sliced
- 1 cup lettuce, shredded
- 4 small tortillas

Steps:

1. Cook pork in a pan over medium heat until cooked through.
2. Stir in taco seasoning and follow packet instructions.
3. Assemble tacos by layering pork, lettuce, and jalapeño slices on tortillas.

Alternatives:

- Use diced chicken for a milder flavor.
- Add a dollop of yogurt to balance the spice.

6. Veggie Fajitas

Serves: 2

Ingredients:

- 1 bell pepper, sliced
- 1 zucchini, sliced
- 1 onion, sliced
- 1 packet fajita seasoning
- 4 small tortillas

Steps:

1. Sauté bell pepper, zucchini, and onion in a pan over medium heat until soft.
2. Stir in fajita seasoning and follow packet instructions.
3. Serve on tortillas.

Alternatives:

- Add mushrooms for an earthy touch.
- Top with sliced olives for extra flavor.

Homemade pizza

1. Classic Margherita Pizza

Serves: 2

Base: Store-bought pizza dough

Ingredients:

- 1 cup marinara sauce
- 1 cup mozzarella cheese, shredded
- A handful of fresh basil leaves
- 1 teaspoon olive oil (optional)

Steps:

1. Preheat oven according to pizza dough package instructions.
2. Roll out the dough on a baking sheet.
3. Spread marinara sauce, sprinkle mozzarella, and scatter basil leaves.
4. Drizzle with olive oil if desired.
5. Bake as per dough instructions or until cheese is melted and golden.

Alternatives:

- Add sliced tomatoes for a fresher take.
- Sprinkle with chili flakes for a kick.

2. BBQ Chicken Tortilla Pizza

Serves: 2

Base: Tortillas

Ingredients:

- 1/2 cup BBQ sauce
- 1 chicken breast, cooked and shredded
- 1/4 cup red onion, thinly sliced
- 1 cup cheddar cheese, shredded

Steps:

1. Preheat oven to 200°C (400°F).
2. Place tortillas on a baking sheet.
3. Spread BBQ sauce, scatter chicken and red onion, and top with cheddar.
4. Bake for 8-10 minutes or until cheese is bubbly.

Alternatives:

- Use mozzarella for a milder cheese flavor.
- Top with fresh cilantro after baking.

3. Veggie Delight Pizza

Serves: 2

Base: Store-bought pizza dough

Ingredients:

- 1 cup marinara sauce
- 1 bell pepper, sliced
- 1/4 cup mushrooms, sliced
- 1/4 cup red onion, sliced
- 1 cup mozzarella cheese, shredded

Steps:

1. Preheat oven as per dough instructions.
2. Roll out the dough on a baking sheet.
3. Spread marinara, sprinkle cheese, and top with veggies.
4. Bake according to dough package or until crust is golden.

Alternatives:

- Add sliced olives or cherry tomatoes for variety.
- Drizzle with garlic oil for extra flavor.

4. Pesto & Feta Tortilla Pizza

Serves: 2

Base: Tortillas

Ingredients:

- 1/2 cup pesto sauce
- 1/4 cup feta cheese, crumbled
- 1/4 cup cherry tomatoes, halved
- 1/4 cup arugula

Steps:

1. Preheat oven to 200°C (400°F).
2. Place tortillas on a baking sheet.
3. Spread pesto, scatter feta, and place cherry tomatoes.
4. Bake for 8-10 minutes or until edges are crisp.
5. Top with fresh arugula before serving.

Alternatives:

- Use mozzarella instead of feta for a creamier texture.
- Add a sprinkle of chili flakes for a spicy kick.

5. Pepperoni & Olive Pizza

Serves: 2

Base: Store-bought pizza dough

Ingredients:

- 1 cup marinara sauce
- 1 cup mozzarella cheese, shredded
- 1/4 cup pepperoni slices
- 1/4 cup black olives, sliced

Steps:

1. Preheat oven according to pizza dough package instructions.
2. Roll out the dough on a baking sheet.
3. Spread marinara, sprinkle cheese, and top with pepperoni and olives.
4. Bake as per dough instructions or until crust is golden.

Alternatives:

- Use green olives for a tangier taste.
- Add sliced jalapeños for extra heat.

Chapter 5

Snacks & Sides

Student life is fast-paced, and sometimes a hearty snack or a side is all you need to refuel and push through. These easy-to-make recipes ensure you have something delicious on hand for when hunger strikes between meals or when you're looking for that perfect complement to your main dish.

DIY Trail Mix

Trail mix: the champion of on-the-go snacking. It's compact, energy-packed, and super customizable. Here's a foundational recipe that's sure to become your favorite study buddy:

Serves: 2

Ingredients:

- 1/2 cup almonds or peanuts (or whatever's on sale!)
- 1/4 cup raisins
- 1/4 cup dried cranberries or dried apricots, chopped
- 2 tablespoons chocolate chips (semi-sweet or milk)
- 2 tablespoons pumpkin seeds or sunflower seeds

Steps:

1. Combine all your ingredients in a mixing bowl.
2. Transfer to an airtight container or split into two zip-lock bags for easy portability.

Alternatives:

- Mix and match with different nuts like walnuts or cashews.
- Not into chocolate chips? Try using M&M's or yogurt-covered raisins.
- Add a savory twist with a sprinkle of sea salt or some roasted chickpeas.

Veggies & dip

1. Simple Hummus

Serves: 2

Ingredients:
- 1 can chickpeas, drained and rinsed
- 2 tablespoons tahini (or peanut butter if on a budget)
- 2 tablespoons olive oil
- 1 garlic clove
- Lemon juice from half a lemon
- Salt to taste
- Water as needed

Steps:
1. Blend chickpeas, tahini, olive oil, garlic, lemon juice, and salt in a blender or food processor.
2. Add water a tablespoon at a time until desired consistency is reached.

Alternatives:
- Add roasted red peppers or olives for a flavor twist.
- Spice it up with a dash of paprika or cumin.

2. Tzatziki

Serves: 2

Ingredients:

- 1 cup Greek yogurt
- Half a cucumber, finely diced
- 1 garlic clove, minced
- 1 tablespoon dill, chopped (or dried dill)
- 1 tablespoon lemon juice
- Salt to taste

Steps:

1. Mix all ingredients in a bowl.
2. Chill in the refrigerator for an hour before serving (if time allows).

Alternatives:

- Add a splash of olive oil for a richer taste.
- Mix in a handful of fresh mint for a refreshing twist.

3. Garlic & Herb Cream Cheese Dip

Serves: 2

Ingredients:

- 1 cup cream cheese, softened
- 1 garlic clove, minced
- 1 tablespoon mixed herbs (parsley, chives, dill, etc.)
- Salt and pepper to taste

Steps:

1. Mix all ingredients in a bowl until well combined.

Alternatives:

- Use a flavored cream cheese as a base for extra zest.
- Add diced olives or sun-dried tomatoes for added flavor.

4. Spicy Salsa

Serves: 2

Ingredients:

- 2 tomatoes, finely chopped
- 1/2 onion, finely chopped
- 1/2 chili pepper, deseeded and finely chopped (adjust to heat preference)
- 1 tablespoon cilantro, chopped
- Lemon juice from half a lemon
- Salt to taste

Steps:

1. Mix all ingredients in a bowl.

Alternatives:

- Add a diced bell pepper for extra crunch.
- Include a dash of cumin or smoked paprika for depth.

5. Avocado Guacamole

Serves: 2

Ingredients:

- 1 ripe avocado
- 1/2 tomato, diced
- 1/4 onion, finely chopped
- Lemon juice from half a lemon
- Salt to taste

Steps:

1. Mash the avocado in a bowl.
2. Mix in the tomato, onion, lemon juice, and salt.

Alternatives:

- Add a touch of garlic or chili for an extra kick.
- Stir in some coriander for a fresh note.

6. Cheesy Queso Dip

Serves: 2

Ingredients:

- 1 cup cheddar cheese, grated
- 1/4 cup milk
- 1/4 teaspoon chili powder (optional)
- Salt to taste

Steps:

1. In a pot on low heat, melt the cheese with milk, stirring continuously.
2. Once melted and smooth, stir in chili powder and salt.

Alternatives:

- Add diced jalapeños for a spicy twist.
- Stir in some salsa for added flavor.

7. Peanut Butter Yogurt Dip

Serves: 2

Ingredients:

- 1 cup Greek yogurt
- 2 tablespoons peanut butter
- 1 tablespoon honey

Steps:

1. Mix all ingredients in a bowl until smooth.

Alternatives:

- Swap peanut butter with almond or cashew butter.
- Drizzle with a bit of chocolate syrup for a dessert-like dip.

Quesadillas

1. Classic Cheese Quesadilla

Serves: 1

Ingredients:

- 2 tortillas (corn or flour)
- 1/2 cup cheddar cheese, shredded
- 2 tablespoons green onions, chopped

Steps:

1. Heat a skillet over medium heat.
2. Place one tortilla in the skillet.
3. Sprinkle the cheese and green onions evenly over the tortilla.
4. Top with the second tortilla and press down gently.
5. Cook for 2-3 minutes on each side until golden brown and cheese is melted.
6. Remove from skillet, let cool for a minute, then cut into wedges and serve.

Alternatives:

- Add some diced tomatoes or bell peppers for added flavor.

2. Chicken & Pepper Quesadilla

Serves: 1

Ingredients:

- 2 tortillas
- 1/2 cup cooked chicken, shredded
- 1/4 cup bell peppers, thinly sliced
- 1/4 cup mozzarella or Monterey Jack cheese, shredded

Steps:

1. Heat a skillet over medium heat.
2. Place one tortilla in the skillet.
3. Layer chicken, bell peppers, and cheese on the tortilla.
4. Top with the second tortilla and press gently.
5. Cook for 2-3 minutes on each side until golden and cheese is melted.
6. Cut into wedges and serve.

Alternatives:

- Add some salsa or hot sauce for a spicy kick.

3. Spinach & Feta Quesadilla

Serves: 1

Ingredients:

- 2 tortillas
- 1/4 cup fresh spinach, chopped
- 1/4 cup feta cheese, crumbled

Steps:

1. Heat a skillet over medium heat.
2. Place one tortilla in the skillet.
3. Sprinkle spinach and feta over the tortilla.
4. Top with the second tortilla and press down gently.
5. Cook for 2-3 minutes on each side until golden brown.
6. Slice and serve.

Alternatives:

- Add some diced tomatoes or olives for extra zest.

4. Black Bean & Corn Quesadilla

Serves: 1

Ingredients:

- 2 tortillas
- 1/4 cup black beans, rinsed and drained
- 1/4 cup corn kernels
- 1/4 cup cheddar cheese, shredded
- 1 tablespoon cilantro, chopped (optional)

Steps:

1. Heat a skillet over medium heat.
2. Place one tortilla in the skillet.
3. Spread black beans, corn, cheese, and cilantro (if using) on the tortilla.
4. Top with the second tortilla and press down gently.
5. Cook for 2-3 minutes on each side until golden and cheese is melted.
6. Slice into wedges and serve.

Alternatives:

- Drizzle with a bit of lime juice for a tangy kick.

Baked sweet potato fries

1. Classic Baked Sweet Potato Fries

Serves: 1

Ingredients:

- 1 large sweet potato, peeled and cut into fries/strips
- 1 tablespoon olive oil
- 1/2 teaspoon salt
- 1/4 teaspoon black pepper

Steps:

1. Preheat oven to 220°C (425°F) and line a baking sheet with parchment paper.
2. In a large bowl, toss sweet potato fries with olive oil, salt, and pepper.
3. Spread the fries in a single layer on the baking sheet, ensuring they aren't crowded.
4. Bake for 20-25 minutes, turning halfway through, or until crispy and golden brown.
5. Remove from the oven and serve immediately.

Alternatives:

- Sprinkle with some grated Parmesan cheese or fresh herbs after baking.

2. Spicy Baked Sweet Potato Fries

Serves: 1

Ingredients:

- 1 large sweet potato, peeled and cut into fries/strips
- 1 tablespoon olive oil
- 1/2 teaspoon salt
- 1/4 teaspoon black pepper
- 1/4 teaspoon smoked paprika
- 1/4 teaspoon cayenne pepper (adjust to taste)

Steps:

1. Preheat oven to 220°C (425°F) and line a baking sheet with parchment paper.
2. In a large bowl, combine sweet potato fries with olive oil, salt, pepper, smoked paprika, and cayenne pepper.
3. Lay out the fries on the baking sheet in a single layer.
4. Bake for 20-25 minutes, turning halfway through, until they are crispy and have a nice golden hue.
5. Once baked, transfer to a serving plate.

Alternatives:

- Serve with a cool yogurt-based dip or aioli to balance the spice.

Chapter 6

Weekend Meals

Weekends are the perfect time to delve a bit deeper into the culinary world. Whether you've had a busy week of lectures or late-night study sessions, now is the time to treat yourself to a more substantial, flavorful meal. Sure, these recipes take a tad longer, but they're well worth the wait. Plus, making a bigger batch means leftovers for the upcoming week!

Easy Chili

Chili is comfort in a bowl, a dish that's rich, hearty, and oh-so-satisfying. It's perfect for weekend cooking, as it can simmer and develop flavors over time. Plus, it freezes beautifully!

1. Classic Beef Chili

Serves: 2

Ingredients:

- 250g ground beef
- 1/2 onion, chopped
- 1 garlic clove, minced
- 1/2 can (200g) diced tomatoes
- 1/2 can (200g) kidney beans, drained and rinsed
- 1 tablespoon tomato paste
- 1/2 teaspoon chili powder (adjust to taste)
- 1/4 teaspoon cumin
- 1/4 teaspoon paprika
- Salt and pepper to taste
- 1/2 cup water or beef broth

Steps:

1. Brown the ground beef in a pot over medium heat. Drain off any excess fat.
2. Add the onion and garlic, cooking until softened.
3. Stir in the tomatoes, beans, tomato paste, and spices.
4. Pour in the water or broth, then bring to a boil.
5. Lower the heat and simmer for 30-40 minutes. Adjust seasoning as needed before serving.

Alternatives:

- Consider adding a handful of diced bell peppers.
- Top with a dollop of sour cream or grated cheese.

2. Chicken Chili

Serves: 2

Ingredients:

- 250g chicken breasts, diced
- 1/2 onion, chopped
- 1 garlic clove, minced
- 1/2 can (200g) diced tomatoes
- 1/2 can (200g) white beans, drained and rinsed
- 1 tablespoon tomato paste
- 1/2 teaspoon chili powder (adjust to taste)
- 1/4 teaspoon oregano
- Salt and pepper to taste
- 1/2 cup chicken broth

Steps:

1. Cook the chicken in a pot until fully browned.
2. Add the onion and garlic, cooking until they soften.
3. Mix in the tomatoes, beans, tomato paste, and spices.
4. Add the chicken broth, bringing everything to a boil.
5. Simmer on low heat for 30-40 minutes, adjusting seasoning before serving.

Alternatives:

- For added color, throw in some chopped spinach in the last 10 minutes of cooking.
- A splash of lime juice can give it a refreshing twist.

Basic Stews & Soups

1. Simple Vegetable Soup

Serves: 2

Ingredients:

- 1 carrot, diced
- 1 potato, diced
- 1/2 onion, chopped
- 1/2 cup frozen peas
- 2 cups vegetable broth
- Salt and pepper
- 1 tablespoon olive oil

Steps:

1. Heat oil in a pot.
2. Add onion; cook until soft.
3. Add carrot, potato, and broth.
4. Boil, then simmer until veggies are soft (about 20 minutes).
5. Stir in peas. Cook 5 more minutes.
6. Add salt and pepper.

Alternatives:

- Swap peas for corn or green beans.
- Add a pinch of garlic powder for extra flavor.

2. Classic Chicken Noodle Soup

Serves: 2

Ingredients:

- 1 chicken breast, diced
- 1 carrot, sliced
- 1 celery stalk, sliced
- 1/2 onion, chopped
- 1 cup egg noodles
- 2 cups chicken broth
- Salt, pepper, and a pinch of thyme
- 1 tablespoon olive oil

Steps:

1. Heat oil in a pot.
2. Cook chicken until no pink shows.
3. Add onion, carrot, celery; cook briefly.
4. Pour in broth; bring to boil.
5. Add noodles. Simmer until soft (about 10 minutes).
6. Season with salt, pepper, and thyme.

Alternatives:

- Use pasta shapes instead of noodles.
- Add a squeeze of lemon for freshness.

3. Tomato Basil Soup

Serves: 2

Ingredients:

- 1 can (400g) diced tomatoes
- 1/2 onion, chopped
- 1 garlic clove, minced
- 2 cups vegetable broth
- A handful of fresh basil, chopped
- Salt and pepper
- 1 tablespoon olive oil

Steps:

1. Heat oil in a pot.
2. Sauté onion and garlic until soft.
3. Add tomatoes and broth; bring to a boil.
4. Simmer for 20 minutes.
5. Blend until smooth, stir in basil, and season.

Alternatives:

- Add some cream for a creamy tomato soup.
- Toss in some chili flakes for a kick.

4. Lentil Soup

Serves: 2

Ingredients:

- 1/2 cup lentils, rinsed
- 1 carrot, diced
- 1/2 onion, chopped
- 2 cups vegetable broth
- Salt and pepper
- 1 tablespoon olive oil

Steps:

1. Heat oil in a pot.
2. Cook onion until soft.
3. Add lentils, carrot, and broth; bring to boil.
4. Simmer until lentils are tender (about 30 minutes).
5. Season to taste.

Alternatives:

- Add some chopped spinach or kale at the end.
- Toss in some cumin for added flavor.

5. Potato Leek Soup

Serves: 2

Ingredients:

- 2 potatoes, diced
- 1 leek, cleaned and sliced
- 2 cups vegetable broth
- Salt and pepper
- 1 tablespoon butter

Steps:

1. Melt butter in a pot.
2. Add leeks; cook until soft.
3. Toss in potatoes and broth; boil.
4. Simmer until potatoes are soft (about 20 minutes).
5. Blend until smooth and season.

Alternatives:

- Garnish with crispy bacon bits.
- Use cream for a richer texture.

6. Broccoli Cheddar Soup

Serves: 2

Ingredients:

- 1 head of broccoli, chopped
- 1/2 onion, chopped
- 1 cup cheddar cheese, grated
- 2 cups vegetable broth
- Salt and pepper
- 1 tablespoon butter

Steps:

1. Melt butter in a pot.
2. Sauté onion until translucent.
3. Add broccoli and broth; boil.
4. Simmer until broccoli is soft (about 15 minutes).
5. Add cheese, stir until melted. Season.

Alternatives:

- Use cauliflower instead of broccoli.
- Add a pinch of nutmeg for depth.

7. *Minestrone Soup*

Serves: 2

Ingredients:

- 1/2 can (200g) diced tomatoes
- 1/2 cup pasta (like elbow or shells)
- 1/2 onion, chopped
- 1 carrot, diced
- 1/2 cup canned beans, drained (like kidney or white beans)
- 2 cups vegetable broth
- Salt, pepper, and dried Italian herbs
- 1 tablespoon olive oil

Steps:

1. Heat oil in a pot.
2. Cook onion and carrot until softened.
3. Add tomatoes, beans, pasta, herbs, and broth; boil.
4. Simmer until pasta is done (about 10 minutes).
5. Season to taste.

Alternatives:

- Add zucchini or green beans for more veggies.
- Garnish with parmesan shavings.

8. Beef Barley Soup

Serves: 2

Ingredients:

- 200g beef chunks, diced
- 1/4 cup barley, rinsed
- 1/2 onion, chopped
- 1 carrot, diced
- 2 cups beef broth
- Salt and pepper
- 1 tablespoon olive oil

Steps:

1. Heat oil in a pot.
2. Brown beef chunks.
3. Add onion and carrot; sauté briefly.
4. Pour in broth, add barley; bring to boil.
5. Simmer until barley is tender (about 40 minutes).
6. Season and serve.

Alternatives:

- Use chicken and chicken broth for a chicken barley soup.
- Add mushrooms for an earthy flavor.

DIY Burgers

1. Basic Beef Burger

Serves: 2

Ingredients:

- 250g ground beef
- 1/2 onion, finely chopped
- Salt and pepper
- 2 burger buns
- Optional toppings: lettuce, tomato, cheese, ketchup

Steps:

1. Mix beef, onion, salt, and pepper in a bowl.
2. Form into 2 patties.
3. Cook on a heated skillet or grill until desired doneness.
4. Assemble on buns with chosen toppings.

Alternatives:

- Add a dash of Worcestershire sauce for flavor.
- Use ground turkey for a leaner option.

2. Spicy Chicken Burger

Serves: 2

Ingredients:

- 250g ground chicken
- 1/2 teaspoon chili powder
- 1/4 teaspoon cumin
- Salt and pepper
- 2 burger buns
- Optional toppings: lettuce, mayo, jalapeños

Steps:

1. Combine chicken, spices, salt, and pepper.
2. Shape into 2 patties.
3. Cook on a skillet or grill until fully cooked.
4. Build your burger with your preferred toppings.

Alternatives:

- Mix in some chopped fresh cilantro.
- Add a slice of pepper jack cheese for extra heat.

3. Simple Veggie Burger

Serves: 2

Ingredients:

- 1 can (400g) black beans, drained and mashed
- 1/2 onion, finely chopped
- 1/4 cup breadcrumbs
- Salt and pepper
- 2 burger buns
- Optional toppings: lettuce, tomato, mustard

Steps:

1. Mix beans, onion, breadcrumbs, salt, and pepper.
2. Form into 2 patties.
3. Cook on a skillet with a bit of oil until crispy on both sides.
4. Assemble your burger as desired.

Alternatives:

- Add a spoon of BBQ sauce for a smoky flavor.
- Use chickpeas instead of black beans.

4. Cheesy Beef Burger

Serves: 2

Ingredients:

- 250g ground beef
- 2 slices of cheddar cheese
- Salt and pepper
- 2 burger buns
- Optional toppings: pickles, onions, ketchup

Steps:

1. Mix beef with salt and pepper.
2. Create 2 patties.
3. Cook on a grill or skillet. Place cheese on patties a minute before done.
4. Serve on buns with chosen toppings.

Alternatives:

- Try blue cheese or Swiss cheese for a change.
- Add bacon strips for extra flavor.

5. Herb Chicken Burger

Serves: 2

Ingredients:

- 250g ground chicken
- 1 tablespoon chopped parsley
- 1/2 teaspoon garlic powder
- Salt and pepper
- 2 burger buns
- Optional toppings: mayo, lettuce, tomato

Steps:

1. Mix chicken, parsley, garlic powder, salt, and pepper.
2. Shape into 2 patties.
3. Cook on a skillet or grill until done.
4. Build your burger as you like.

Alternatives:

- Use fresh basil instead of parsley.
- Add avocado slices for creaminess.

6. Mushroom Veggie Burger

Serves: 2

Ingredients:

- 1 cup finely chopped mushrooms
- 1/2 cup cooked quinoa
- 1/4 cup breadcrumbs
- Salt and pepper
- 2 burger buns
- Optional toppings: Swiss cheese, mayo, arugula

Steps:

1. Mix mushrooms, quinoa, breadcrumbs, salt, and pepper.
2. Form into 2 patties.
3. Cook on a skillet until both sides are golden.
4. Assemble with your favorite toppings.

Alternatives:

- Add a dash of soy sauce for depth.
- Use brown rice instead of quinoa.

7. BBQ Beef Burger

Serves: 2

Ingredients:

- 250g ground beef
- 2 tablespoons BBQ sauce
- Salt and pepper
- 2 burger buns
- Optional toppings: onion rings, lettuce, more BBQ sauce

Steps:

1. Combine beef, BBQ sauce, salt, and pepper.
2. Make 2 patties.
3. Cook on a grill or skillet until your preferred doneness.
4. Stack on buns with chosen toppings.

Alternatives:

- Add smoked paprika for a deeper flavor.
- Top with coleslaw for a crunch.

8. Asian-style Chicken Burger

Serves: 2

Ingredients:

- 250g ground chicken
- 1 tablespoon teriyaki sauce
- 2 green onions, chopped
- 2 burger buns
- Optional toppings: pickled ginger, mayo, lettuce

Steps:

1. Mix chicken, teriyaki sauce, and green onions.
2. Shape into 2 patties.
3. Cook on a skillet or grill until fully cooked.
4. Assemble burgers with toppings of choice.

Alternatives:

- Add a slice of pineapple for a tropical twist.
- Use hoisin sauce instead of teriyaki.

Casseroles

1. Classic Tuna Pasta Casserole

Serves: 2

Ingredients:

- 1 cup pasta (like elbow or penne)
- 1 can (185g) tuna, drained
- 1/2 onion, chopped
- 1 can (295g) cream of mushroom soup
- 1/2 cup frozen peas
- 1/2 cup grated cheddar cheese
- Salt and pepper to taste
- 1 tablespoon olive oil

Steps:

1. Preheat oven to 200°C (400°F).
2. Cook pasta as per package directions, drain.
3. In a pan, sauté onions in olive oil until translucent.
4. In a bowl, mix pasta, tuna, onions, mushroom soup, peas, salt, and pepper.
5. Transfer to a baking dish and top with cheese.
6. Bake for 20-25 minutes until bubbly and golden on top.

Alternatives:

- Use canned chicken instead of tuna.
- Add bell peppers or corn for extra veggies.

2. Cheesy Potato & Sausage Casserole

Serves: 2

Ingredients:

- 2 potatoes, thinly sliced
- 2 sausages, sliced
- 1/2 onion, chopped
- 1 cup grated cheese (like cheddar or mozzarella)
- 1 cup milk
- 1 tablespoon butter
- Salt, pepper, and a pinch of paprika

Steps:

1. Preheat oven to 200°C (400°F).
2. In a pan, sauté onions and sausages in butter until onions are soft and sausages are slightly browned.
3. In a baking dish, layer half the potatoes, then half the sausage mixture, and then half the cheese. Repeat layers.
4. Pour milk over the layers, and season with salt, pepper, and paprika.
5. Bake for 40-45 minutes, or until potatoes are tender.

Alternatives:

- Swap sausages for diced chicken or ham.
- Mix in some chopped spinach or kale for greens.

3. Veggie Rice Casserole

Serves: 2

Ingredients:

- 1 cup cooked rice
- 1/2 cup broccoli florets
- 1/2 cup bell pepper, diced
- 1/2 can (200g) diced tomatoes, drained
- 1/2 cup grated cheese (like cheddar or feta)
- 1/2 onion, chopped
- 1 garlic clove, minced
- Salt, pepper, and a pinch of dried oregano
- 1 tablespoon olive oil

Steps:

1. Preheat oven to 200°C (400°F).
2. In a pan, sauté onion and garlic in olive oil until soft. Add bell pepper and sauté for another 3 minutes.
3. In a bowl, combine rice, broccoli, sautéed veggies, tomatoes, half the cheese, salt, pepper, and oregano.
4. Transfer to a baking dish, top with remaining cheese.
5. Bake for 20-25 minutes until cheese is melted and slightly golden.

Alternatives:

- Incorporate some cooked beans or lentils for added protein.
- Use quinoa instead of rice for a variation.

Slow Cooker Recipes

1. Basic Pulled Pork

Serves: 2

Ingredients:

- 500g pork shoulder
- 1 cup BBQ sauce
- 1/2 onion, chopped
- 1/2 cup chicken broth
- Salt and pepper

Steps:

1. Season pork with salt and pepper.
2. Place all ingredients in the slow cooker.
3. Cook on low for 8 hours.
4. Shred pork with two forks and stir.

Alternatives:

- Use beef brisket for pulled beef.
- Add a dash of smoked paprika for a smokier flavor.

2. Veggie Cacciatore

Serves: 2

Ingredients:

- 2 bell peppers, sliced
- 1 zucchini, sliced
- 1/2 onion, chopped
- 1 can (400g) diced tomatoes
- 1 garlic clove, minced
- 1 teaspoon dried oregano
- Salt and pepper

Steps:

1. Place all ingredients in the slow cooker.
2. Cook on low for 6 hours.
3. Stir and adjust seasoning.

Alternatives:

- Add sliced mushrooms or eggplant.
- Sprinkle with grated Parmesan before serving.

3. Chicken Curry

Serves: 2

Ingredients:

- 2 chicken breasts
- 1 can (400ml) coconut milk
- 2 tablespoons curry powder
- 1/2 onion, chopped
- 1/2 cup peas
- Salt and pepper

Steps:

1. Place chicken, onion, coconut milk, curry powder, salt, and pepper in the slow cooker.
2. Cook on low for 6 hours.
3. Add peas, cook for another 30 minutes.
4. Adjust seasoning and serve.

Alternatives:

- Use tofu instead of chicken for a vegetarian option.
- Stir in some spinach at the end for added greens.

4. Beef Stew

Serves: 2

Ingredients:

- 250g beef chunks
- 2 carrots, sliced
- 2 potatoes, diced
- 1/2 onion, chopped
- 2 cups beef broth
- 1 teaspoon dried thyme
- Salt and pepper

Steps:

1. Place all ingredients in the slow cooker.
2. Cook on low for 8 hours.
3. Stir, adjust seasoning, and serve.

Alternatives:

- Add green beans or peas in the last hour of cooking.
- Use a dash of Worcestershire sauce for added depth.

5. Bean Chili

Serves: 2

Ingredients:

- 1 can (400g) red kidney beans, drained
- 1/2 can (200g) diced tomatoes
- 1 bell pepper, chopped
- 1/2 onion, chopped
- 1 tablespoon chili powder
- Salt and pepper

Steps:

1. Mix all ingredients in the slow cooker.
2. Cook on low for 6 hours.
3. Stir, adjust seasoning, and serve.

Alternatives:

- Add ground beef or turkey for a meaty version.
- Serve with a dollop of sour cream or shredded cheese.

6. Creamy Garlic Chicken

Serves: 2

Ingredients:

- 2 chicken breasts
- 1/2 cup cream or milk
- 2 garlic cloves, minced
- 1/2 onion, chopped
- Salt and pepper

Steps:

1. Place chicken, garlic, onion, salt, and pepper in the slow cooker.
2. Cook on low for 6 hours.
3. Stir in cream or milk, cook for another 30 minutes.
4. Adjust seasoning and serve.

Alternatives:

- Sprinkle with parsley or dill before serving.
- Use mushrooms for an earthy flavor.

7. Spaghetti Bolognese

Serves: 2

Ingredients:

- 250g ground beef or turkey
- 1 can (400g) crushed tomatoes
- 1/2 onion, finely chopped
- 1 garlic clove, minced
- 1 teaspoon dried basil
- 1 teaspoon dried oregano
- Salt and pepper

Steps:

1. Brown the ground beef in a pan, then transfer to the slow cooker.
2. Add all other ingredients and stir.
3. Cook on low for 6-7 hours.
4. Serve over cooked spaghetti.

Alternatives:

- Add some red wine for depth of flavor.
- Stir in cooked mushrooms or bell peppers for more veggies.

8. Sausage & Bean Casserole

Serves: 2

Ingredients:

- 2 sausages, sliced
- 1 can (400g) white beans, drained
- 1/2 onion, chopped
- 1/2 bell pepper, chopped
- 1/2 can (200g) diced tomatoes
- 1 teaspoon smoked paprika
- Salt and pepper

Steps:

1. Place all ingredients in the slow cooker.
2. Cook on low for 6 hours.
3. Stir and adjust seasoning before serving.

Alternatives:

- Use chorizo for a spicier kick.
- Add kale or spinach for added greens.

9. Coconut Lentil Curry

Serves: 2

Ingredients:

- 1 cup lentils, rinsed
- 1 can (400ml) coconut milk
- 1/2 onion, chopped
- 1 tablespoon curry powder
- Salt and pepper
- 2 cups water or vegetable broth

Steps:

1. Combine all ingredients in the slow cooker.
2. Cook on low for 7-8 hours.
3. Stir and adjust seasoning before serving.

Alternatives:

- Add diced carrots or potatoes.
- Stir in spinach at the end for added nutrition.

10. BBQ Pulled Chicken

Serves: 2

Ingredients:

- 2 chicken breasts
- 1 cup BBQ sauce
- 1/2 onion, sliced
- 1/4 cup chicken broth
- Salt and pepper

Steps:

1. Mix BBQ sauce, onion, chicken broth, salt, and pepper in the slow cooker.
2. Add chicken breasts and ensure they're well-coated.
3. Cook on low for 7 hours.
4. Shred chicken with two forks and mix well before serving.

Alternatives:

- Serve over rice or inside sandwich buns.
- Add a dash of hot sauce for extra heat.

11. Creamy Mushroom & Chicken

Serves: 2

Ingredients:

- 2 chicken breasts
- 1 cup mushrooms, sliced
- 1 can (295g) cream of mushroom soup
- 1/2 onion, chopped
- Salt and pepper

Steps:

1. Place all ingredients in the slow cooker.
2. Cook on low for 6-7 hours.
3. Stir and adjust seasoning before serving.

Alternatives:

- Serve over rice or mashed potatoes.
- Use thighs instead of breasts for a richer flavor.

Curries from Scratch

Embarking on the journey of making curries from scratch is like taking a deep dive into the vast ocean of flavors, spices, and culinary techniques. While the quick curries offered convenience and speed, these recipes allow you to embrace the full essence of traditional cooking. Perfect for a weekend project or to impress on a date night, these curries will expand your culinary horizons and enrich your taste buds. Yes, they require a bit more effort, but trust us, the aromatic symphony and the depth of flavors are totally worth it!

Tips for Making Curries from Scratch:

- Gather All Ingredients: Before starting, ensure you have all the ingredients on hand. Traditional curries often involve a long list of spices and herbs.
- Use Fresh Spices: Freshly ground spices (like cumin, coriander, and cardamom) can elevate the flavor profile immensely.
- Taste As You Go: The beauty of curries is that they're adaptable. Feel free to adjust the seasoning to suit your preference.
- Patience is Key: Let the curry simmer and allow the ingredients to meld together. The longer it simmers, the richer the flavor.
- Serve with Love: Curries are best enjoyed with a side of rice, naan, or roti. And always, always share with someone, because good food is best enjoyed in good company.

1. Chicken Tikka Masala

Serves: 2

Ingredients:

- 2 chicken breasts, cubed
- 1 cup yogurt (optional)
- 3 tomatoes, puréed (or a can of tomato sauce)
- 1 onion, finely chopped
- 2 garlic cloves, minced
- 1-inch ginger, grated
- 2 teaspoons garam masala
- 1 teaspoon turmeric
- 1 teaspoon cumin
- 1 teaspoon paprika
- 1/2 teaspoon red chili powder (optional, for heat)
- 2 tablespoons cream (or milk)
- 2 tablespoons oil
- Salt to taste
- Fresh cilantro for garnish (optional, or use dried coriander)

Steps:

1. In a pan, heat oil and sauté onions until translucent. Add ginger and garlic.
2. Add the chicken and brown slightly on all sides.
3. Pour in the tomato purée, followed by all the spices, yogurt, and salt.
4. Let it simmer for 20 minutes.
5. Stir in cream or milk for a richer texture.
6. Garnish with cilantro or dried coriander and serve.

Alternatives:

- Substitute chicken with tofu or chickpeas.
- For creaminess, canned coconut milk can be used instead of cream.

2. Lamb Rogan Josh

Serves: 2

Ingredients:

- 250g lamb, diced (or beef)
- 1 onion, finely chopped
- 2 garlic cloves, minced
- 1-inch ginger, grated
- 2 teaspoons ground fennel (or anise seed)
- 1 teaspoon ground cinnamon
- 1 teaspoon ground cumin
- 1 teaspoon paprika
- 1/2 teaspoon red chili powder (optional)
- 2 tablespoons yogurt (optional, can be omitted)
- 2 tablespoons oil
- Salt to taste

Steps:

1. In a pan, heat oil and sauté onions until golden. Add ginger and garlic.
2. Add the lamb or beef and brown all sides.
3. Mix in the spices and yogurt.
4. Let it simmer for 40 minutes until the meat is tender.
5. Serve hot.

Alternatives:

- Use chicken or beef if lamb is not available or expensive.
- For a richer flavor, a splash of tomato sauce can be added.

3. Beef Vindaloo

Serves: 2

Ingredients:

- 250g beef, diced
- 2 dried red chilies (or 1 tsp chili flakes)
- 1 teaspoon mustard seeds
- 1 teaspoon cumin seeds
- 1/2 teaspoon turmeric
- 1 onion, chopped
- 2 garlic cloves, minced
- 1-inch ginger, grated
- 2 tablespoons vinegar (or lemon juice)
- 2 tablespoons oil
- Salt to taste

Steps:

1. In a pan, heat oil and sauté onions. Add ginger and garlic.
2. Add the beef and brown all sides.
3. Mix in the spices, vinegar, and chili.
4. Let it simmer for 45 minutes until the meat is tender.
5. Serve hot.

Alternatives:

- Substitute beef with chicken or pork.
- If you don't have vinegar, use lime or lemon juice.

4. Vegetable Korma

Serves: 2

Ingredients:

- 1 cup mixed vegetables (like frozen vegetable mix)
- 1/2 cup coconut milk (or regular milk with a pinch of coconut flavoring)
- 1 onion, chopped
- 1 garlic clove, minced
- 1-inch ginger, grated
- 1 teaspoon garam masala
- 1/2 teaspoon turmeric
- 1/2 teaspoon cumin
- 1/4 cup cashews (optional)
- 2 tablespoons oil
- Salt to taste
- Fresh cilantro for garnish (optional, or dried coriander)

Steps:

1. In a pan, heat oil and sauté onions. Add ginger and garlic.
2. Add the vegetables and sauté for a few minutes.
3. Pour in coconut milk, followed by the spices, cashews, and salt.
4. Let it simmer for 15 minutes.
5. Garnish with cilantro or dried coriander and serve.

Alternatives:

- Substitute any vegetables with what you have on hand or prefer.
- Use almonds instead of cashews.

5. Thai Green Chicken Curry

Serves: 2

Ingredients:

- 2 chicken breasts, sliced
- 1 can (400ml) coconut milk
- 2 tablespoons green curry paste (store-bought for convenience)
- 1 bell pepper, sliced
- 1 small zucchini, sliced
- 1 tablespoon fish sauce (or soy sauce)
- 1 tablespoon brown sugar
- 2 tablespoons oil
- Fresh basil leaves for garnish (optional)
- 1 lime, wedged

Steps:

1. In a pan, heat oil and sauté the chicken slices until lightly browned.
2. Add the green curry paste and stir for a minute.
3. Pour in the coconut milk, followed by bell pepper and zucchini.
4. Add the fish sauce and brown sugar. Let it simmer for 15-20 minutes.
5. Serve with a garnish of basil leaves and a wedge of lime on the side.

Alternatives:

- Use tofu or prawns instead of chicken.
- Add other vegetables like snap peas or bamboo shoots.

6. Thai Red Curry with Beef

Serves: 2

Ingredients:

- 250g beef, thinly sliced
- 1 can (400ml) coconut milk
- 2 tablespoons red curry paste (store-bought)
- 1 cup Thai eggplants or green beans, cut
- 1 tablespoon fish sauce (or soy sauce)
- 1 tablespoon brown sugar
- 2 tablespoons oil
- Fresh Thai basil (optional)

Steps:

1. Heat oil in a pan. Add the beef and brown it.
2. Stir in the red curry paste.
3. Add the coconut milk, vegetables, fish sauce, and brown sugar.
4. Simmer until beef is tender and vegetables are cooked, about 20 minutes.
5. Garnish with Thai basil if available.

Alternatives:

- Use chicken, pork, or tofu instead of beef.
- Add baby corn or bamboo shoots for variety.

7. Moroccan Lamb Curry

Serves: 2

Ingredients:

- 250g lamb, diced
- 1 onion, chopped
- 2 garlic cloves, minced
- 1-inch ginger, grated
- 1 teaspoon ground cumin
- 1 teaspoon ground coriander
- 1/2 teaspoon ground cinnamon
- 1/4 teaspoon cayenne pepper
- 1 can diced tomatoes (400ml)
- 1/4 cup raisins or dried apricots, chopped
- 2 tablespoons oil
- Salt to taste
- Fresh coriander for garnish (optional)

Steps:

1. In a pan, heat oil and brown the lamb pieces.
2. Add onions, garlic, and ginger. Sauté until onions are translucent.
3. Mix in the spices, followed by the tomatoes.
4. Add raisins or apricots. Cover and let it simmer for about 40 minutes until the lamb is tender.
5. Garnish with fresh coriander and serve.

Alternatives:

- Use beef or chicken instead of lamb.
- Add chickpeas for extra protein and texture.

8. Japanese Curry with Pork

Serves: 2

Ingredients:

- 250g pork, thinly sliced or cubed
- 2 potatoes, diced
- 1 carrot, diced
- 1 onion, chopped
- 2-3 blocks of Japanese curry roux (store-bought)
- 500ml water
- 2 tablespoons oil
- Pickled ginger for garnish (optional)

Steps:

1. Heat oil in a pot and brown the pork slices.
2. Add onions, carrots, and potatoes. Sauté for a few minutes.
3. Pour in the water and bring to a boil. Reduce the heat and let it simmer until the vegetables are half done.
4. Add the curry roux blocks and stir until dissolved.
5. Simmer until the pork and vegetables are fully cooked and the curry thickens.
6. Serve with a side of pickled ginger.

Alternatives:

- Substitute pork with chicken, beef, or tofu.
- Add bell peppers or peas for a different flavor profile.

Chapter 7

Fakeaway - Your Fave UK Takeaways Reimagined

Craving that spicy kick from "Fernando's" or perhaps the noodly goodness of "Wok-a-mama"? Fret not! Dive into these homemade versions of UK's beloved takeaways. Less waiting, more eating, and, most importantly, no delivery charge!

1. Fernando's Fiery Grilled Chicken

Serves: 2

Ingredients:

- 2 chicken breasts
- 2 tablespoons peri-peri sauce (store-bought for convenience)
- 1 tablespoon lemon juice
- 1 tablespoon oil
- Salt and pepper to taste

Steps:

1. Mix peri-peri sauce, lemon juice, oil, salt, and pepper in a bowl.
2. Marinate chicken breasts in the mixture for at least 30 minutes (longer for more flavour).
3. Grill on a pan over medium heat for 6-7 minutes on each side or until fully cooked.
4. Serve hot with a side of your choice.

Alternatives:

- Can also be cooked in an oven at 200°C for around 20 minutes.
- For added heat, sprinkle some chili flakes on top!

2. Cheeky Chicken Wings

Serves: 2

Ingredients:

- 10 chicken wings
- 2 tablespoons peri-peri sauce
- 1 tablespoon honey
- Salt to taste

Steps:

1. Mix peri-peri sauce, honey, and salt in a bowl.
2. Toss chicken wings in the mixture.
3. Lay them out on a baking tray.
4. Bake at 200°C for 25-30 minutes or until crispy.
5. Serve with a dipping sauce or as is for a spicy treat.

Alternatives:

- Can also be grilled or fried for a different texture.
- Add a sprinkle of garlic powder for added flavour.

3. Spicy Bean Burger (Veggie option)

Serves: 2

Ingredients:

- 1 can black beans, drained and mashed
- 1/2 onion, finely chopped
- 2 cloves garlic, minced
- 2 tablespoons peri-peri sauce
- 1/2 cup breadcrumbs
- Salt and pepper to taste
- 2 burger buns and toppings of your choice

Steps:

1. Mix mashed beans, onion, garlic, peri-peri sauce, breadcrumbs, salt, and pepper in a bowl.
2. Form into two patties.
3. Grill on a pan over medium heat for 4-5 minutes on each side.
4. Assemble your burger with your desired toppings and enjoy!

Alternatives:

- Add a slice of cheese on top while grilling for a cheesy delight.
- Use chickpeas or lentils instead of black beans.

4. Peri-Peri Corn on the Cob

Serves: 2

Ingredients:

- 2 corn on the cobs
- 2 tablespoons butter, melted
- 1 tablespoon peri-peri sauce
- A pinch of salt

Steps:

1. Mix melted butter, peri-peri sauce, and salt in a bowl.
2. Brush this mixture over the corn cobs.
3. Grill them on a pan or oven at 200°C for about 15 minutes, turning occasionally.
4. Serve hot with a sprinkle of chili flakes if you like it extra spicy!

Alternatives:

- Use peri-peri mayo as a dipping sauce.
- For a smoky flavor, add a sprinkle of smoked paprika.

Wok-a-mama's

1. Wok-a-mama's Classic Ramen

Serves: 2

Ingredients:

- 2 packets instant ramen noodles
- 800ml chicken or vegetable broth
- 1 tablespoon soy sauce
- 1 tablespoon miso paste (optional)
- 2 garlic cloves, minced
- 1-inch ginger, grated
- 2 spring onions, chopped
- 100g cooked chicken slices or tofu cubes
- 1 boiled egg, halved
- Nori (seaweed) sheets, and sesame seeds for garnish

Steps:

1. In a pot, sauté garlic and ginger until fragrant.
2. Add broth, soy sauce, and miso paste. Bring to a simmer.
3. In a separate pot, cook ramen noodles as per the packet instructions.
4. Divide the cooked noodles between two bowls.
5. Pour the simmering broth over the noodles.
6. Top with chicken or tofu, boiled egg, spring onions, and garnish with nori and sesame seeds.

Alternatives:

- Add vegetables like bok choy, corn, or spinach.
- Use beef or pork slices instead of chicken.

2. Quickie Stir-fry Noodles

Serves: 2

Ingredients:

- 200g rice noodles or any available noodles
- 1 bell pepper, julienned
- 1 carrot, julienned
- 2 spring onions, sliced
- 1 tablespoon soy sauce
- 1 tablespoon oyster sauce (or hoisin sauce)
- 2 cloves garlic, minced
- 1 tablespoon oil

Steps:

1. Prepare noodles as per package instructions.
2. In a wok or pan, heat oil and sauté garlic.
3. Add bell pepper and carrot, stir-frying until slightly tender.
4. Toss in the cooked noodles, soy sauce, and oyster sauce.
5. Stir-fry for a couple of minutes until all is well combined.
6. Garnish with spring onions.

Alternatives:

- Add proteins like chicken, beef, or tofu.
- Throw in more veggies like snow peas or mushrooms.

3. Spicy Coconut Curry

Serves: 2

Ingredients:

- 1 can (400ml) coconut milk
- 200g tofu cubes or chicken pieces
- 1 tablespoon red curry paste (store-bought for ease)
- 1 bell pepper, sliced
- 1 small zucchini, sliced
- 1 tablespoon oil

Steps:

1. In a wok or pot, heat oil and sauté the curry paste for a minute.
2. Pour in the coconut milk, stirring to combine.
3. Add tofu or chicken and let it simmer for 10 minutes.
4. Throw in the bell pepper and zucchini and cook for another 10 minutes.
5. Serve hot with rice or noodles.

Alternatives:

- Opt for green curry paste for a different flavor.
- Add bamboo shoots or baby corn for variety.

4. Tofu Teriyaki Bowl

Serves: 2

Ingredients:

- 200g firm tofu, cubed
- 2 cups cooked rice
- 3 tablespoons teriyaki sauce (store-bought)
- 1 tablespoon sesame seeds
- 1 spring onion, sliced
- 1 tablespoon oil

Steps:

1. In a pan, heat oil and fry tofu cubes until golden.
2. Pour teriyaki sauce over the tofu, letting it simmer for a couple of minutes.
3. Serve the teriyaki tofu over cooked rice.
4. Garnish with sesame seeds and spring onions.

Alternatives:

- Use chicken or beef strips instead of tofu.
- Add a side of sautéed veggies like bell peppers or snap peas.

Mackie D's

1. Mackie's Classic Burger

Serves: 2

Ingredients:

- 2 beef patties (can be store-bought for convenience)
- 2 burger buns
- 2 slices cheddar cheese
- 4 lettuce leaves
- 1 tomato, sliced
- 2 tablespoons mayo
- 1 small onion, sliced
- Salt and pepper
- 1 tablespoon oil for frying

Steps:

1. Heat oil in a pan over medium heat. Season the beef patties with salt and pepper.
2. Fry patties for about 4 minutes each side or until desired doneness.
3. Just before removing from the pan, place a cheese slice on each patty to melt slightly.
4. Toast the buns lightly.
5. Assemble the burger: Start with mayo on the bottom bun, followed by lettuce, tomato, beef patty with cheese, and onion. Top with the other half of the bun.
6. Serve with a side of your choice.

Alternatives:

- Add pickles or switch out mayo for mustard.
- Use a chicken patty or veggie patty instead.

2. Crispy Chicken Sandwich

Serves: 2

Ingredients:

- 2 chicken breasts
- 1 cup breadcrumbs
- 1 egg, beaten
- 2 burger buns
- 4 lettuce leaves
- 2 tablespoons mayo
- Salt and pepper
- Oil for frying

Steps:

1. Dip each chicken breast in the beaten egg and then coat with breadcrumbs.
2. Heat oil in a frying pan and fry chicken until golden and cooked through.
3. Toast the buns lightly.
4. Assemble the sandwich with mayo, lettuce, and the crispy chicken breast.
5. Serve hot.

Alternatives:

- Add a slice of cheese or some pickles.
- Use a spicy mayo or hot sauce for a kick.

3. Mackie's Veggie Delight Wrap

Serves: 2

Ingredients:

- 2 large tortilla wraps
- 1 cup mixed salad greens
- 1 tomato, diced
- 1/2 cucumber, diced
- 1/4 cup grated cheddar cheese
- 2 tablespoons ranch dressing or any preferred sauce
- Salt and pepper

Steps:

1. Lay out the tortilla wraps.
2. Spread the dressing or sauce in the middle.
3. Place the salad greens, diced tomato, and cucumber on the sauce.
4. Sprinkle with grated cheese, salt, and pepper.
5. Roll up the tortilla, tucking in the sides as you go.
6. Serve as is or cut in half.

Alternatives:

- Add some grilled chicken or crispy tofu for protein.
- Switch out the dressing for hummus or tzatziki.

4. Mackie's Apple Pie Turnover

Serves: 2

Ingredients:

- 1 apple, peeled and diced
- 2 tablespoons sugar
- 1/2 teaspoon cinnamon
- 2 squares of ready-made puff pastry
- 1 egg, beaten (for brushing)

Steps:

1. Preheat oven to 200°C (400°F).
2. In a bowl, mix diced apple with sugar and cinnamon.
3. Place half of the apple mixture in the center of each puff pastry square.
4. Fold the pastry over the apple mixture, forming a triangle. Press edges to seal.
5. Brush the turnovers with the beaten egg.
6. Bake in the preheated oven for 15-20 minutes or until golden brown.
7. Serve warm.

Alternatives:

- Use berries or a mix of fruits.
- Serve with a dollop of ice cream or custard.

Starbeans

You will need a cafetière (also known as a French press) for these recipes!

1. Starbeans Classic Brew

Serves: 1

Ingredients:

- 2 tablespoons coarse coffee grounds
- 1 cup boiling water
- Milk or creamer to taste
- Sugar or sweetener to taste

Steps:

1. Add the coffee grounds to your cafetière.
2. Pour in the boiling water.
3. Place the lid on, but don't press down yet. Let it steep for 4 minutes.
4. Press down slowly, then pour into your mug.
5. Add milk or creamer and sugar as desired.

Alternatives:

- Add a cinnamon stick or vanilla pod to the cafetière for a flavorful twist.

2. Starbeans Iced Coffee Blend

Serves: 1

Ingredients:

- 2 tablespoons coarse coffee grounds
- 1 cup cold water
- Ice cubes
- Milk or creamer to taste
- Sugar syrup or sweetener to taste

Steps:

1. Add coffee grounds to the cafetière.
2. Pour in cold water.
3. Place in the refrigerator and let steep for 12-15 hours.
4. Press down slowly and pour over a glass filled with ice.
5. Add milk or creamer and sugar syrup as desired.

Alternatives:

- Garnish with a slice of orange or lemon for a citrusy kick.

3. Starbeans Chocolate Dream

Serves: 1

Ingredients:

- 2 tablespoons coarse coffee grounds
- 1 tablespoon cocoa powder
- 1 cup boiling water
- Milk or creamer to taste
- Sugar or sweetener to taste

Steps:

1. Mix coffee grounds and cocoa powder in the cafetière.
2. Add boiling water and let it steep for 5 minutes.
3. Press down slowly and pour into a mug.
4. Add milk or creamer and sugar as desired.

Alternatives:

- Add a pinch of chili powder for a spicy kick.

4. *Starbeans Coconut Bliss*

Serves: 1

Ingredients:

- 2 tablespoons coarse coffee grounds
- 1 cup boiling water
- 1 tablespoon coconut oil

Steps:

1. Add coffee grounds to the cafetière.
2. Pour boiling water and allow to steep for 4 minutes.
3. Press down slowly and pour coffee into a blender.
4. Add coconut oil and blend until frothy.
5. Serve immediately.

Alternatives:

- Sprinkle with toasted coconut flakes for added texture.

5. Starbeans Honey Almond Delight

Serves: 1

Ingredients:

- 2 tablespoons coarse coffee grounds
- 1 cup boiling water
- 1 tablespoon honey
- A splash of almond extract

Steps:

1. Brew coffee in the cafetière for 4 minutes.
2. Press down and pour into your mug.
3. Stir in honey and a splash of almond extract.

Alternatives:

- Top with whipped cream and slivered almonds.

6. *Starbeans Herbal Fusion*

Serves: 1

Ingredients:

- 2 tablespoons coarse coffee grounds
- 1 cup boiling water
- 1 sprig of fresh mint or lavender

Steps:

1. Place coffee grounds and your choice of herb in the cafetière.
2. Pour boiling water and steep for 5 minutes.
3. Press down slowly and pour into your mug.

Alternatives:

- Sweeten with agave nectar or maple syrup for a different flavor profile.

Pret a Almost's

1. Classic Chicken Caesar Wrap

Serves: 1

Ingredients:

- 1 large tortilla wrap
- 1 grilled chicken breast, sliced
- 2 tablespoons Caesar dressing
- 1/4 cup romaine lettuce, shredded
- 2 tablespoons grated Parmesan cheese
- 1 tablespoon croutons, crushed

Steps:

1. Spread the Caesar dressing over the tortilla.
2. Layer on the shredded romaine lettuce.
3. Place the sliced grilled chicken over the lettuce.
4. Sprinkle the Parmesan cheese and crushed croutons.
5. Roll up the tortilla, cut in half, and serve.

Alternatives:

- Add some sliced avocados for creaminess.

2. Tuna Nicoise Sandwich

Serves: 1

Ingredients:

- 2 slices of whole grain bread
- 1 small can of tuna in brine, drained
- 1 tablespoon mayonnaise
- 1 teaspoon Dijon mustard
- 2 slices of tomato
- 1 hard-boiled egg, sliced
- 3-4 black olives, chopped

Steps:

1. Mix tuna, mayonnaise, and Dijon mustard in a bowl.
2. Spread the tuna mixture on one slice of bread.
3. Layer on tomato slices, egg slices, and chopped olives.
4. Top with the second slice of bread and serve.

Alternatives:

- Add a few capers for an extra burst of flavor.

3. Vegetarian Avo & Hummus Baguette

Serves: 1

Ingredients:

- 1 mini baguette or half a regular-sized one, sliced open
- 2 tablespoons hummus
- 1/2 ripe avocado, sliced
- 1/4 cup mixed salad greens
- 1 tablespoon sun-dried tomatoes, chopped

Steps:

1. Spread hummus on the bottom slice of the baguette.
2. Place avocado slices on top.
3. Add salad greens and sun-dried tomatoes.
4. Close with the top half of the baguette and serve.

Alternatives:

- Sprinkle some feta cheese for added tang.

4. Vegan Falafel & Tzatziki Wrap

Serves: 1

Ingredients:

- 1 large tortilla wrap
- 3 falafel balls, crushed
- 2 tablespoons tzatziki (use vegan versions available in stores)
- 1/4 cup shredded lettuce
- 1 tablespoon diced cucumber
- 1 tablespoon diced tomato

Steps:

1. Spread the tzatziki over the tortilla.
2. Add the crushed falafel.
3. Layer on lettuce, cucumber, and tomato.
4. Roll up the tortilla, cut in half, and serve.

Alternatives:

- Add some chopped mint for freshness.

5. Pret a Almost's Porridge with Berries & Honey

Serves: 1

Ingredients:

- 1/2 cup rolled oats
- 1 cup milk (dairy or plant-based)
- 1/4 cup mixed berries (like strawberries, blueberries)
- 1 tablespoon honey or maple syrup

Steps:

1. In a saucepan, heat the milk until it's steaming.
2. Add the rolled oats and stir.
3. Simmer on low heat for 5-7 minutes, stirring occasionally until thickened.
4. Transfer to a bowl, top with berries, and drizzle with honey or maple syrup.

Alternatives:

- Add some chia seeds or nuts for added texture.

GFC

1. GFC's Classic Fried Chicken Drumstick

Serves: 2

Ingredients:

- 4 chicken drumsticks
- 2 cups buttermilk (or 2 cups milk + 2 tsp vinegar, mixed and set for 10 mins)
- 2 cups all-purpose flour
- 1 teaspoon paprika
- 1 teaspoon garlic powder
- 1 teaspoon onion powder
- Salt and pepper to taste
- Vegetable oil for frying

Steps:

1. In a bowl, soak the chicken drumsticks in the buttermilk for at least 30 minutes. This makes the chicken tender.
2. In another bowl, combine the flour, paprika, garlic powder, onion powder, salt, and pepper.
3. Heat the vegetable oil in a deep frying pan over medium heat.
4. Take each drumstick, let the excess buttermilk drip off, and then roll in the flour mixture until well coated.
5. Carefully place the coated drumsticks in the hot oil.
6. Fry for about 15 minutes, turning occasionally, until golden brown and cooked through.
7. Remove from oil and drain on paper towels.

8. Serve with your favorite dipping sauce.

Alternatives:

- For a spicier kick, add a teaspoon of cayenne pepper to the flour mixture.
- Swap out drumsticks for chicken wings or tenders.

2. GFC's Crispy Chicken Burger

Serves: 2

Ingredients:

- 2 boneless chicken breasts
- 1 cup buttermilk
- 1 cup all-purpose flour
- 1 teaspoon ground black pepper
- 1 teaspoon garlic powder
- Vegetable oil for frying
- 2 burger buns
- Lettuce, tomato, mayo for toppings

Steps:

1. Pound the chicken breasts slightly to even thickness.
2. Soak them in buttermilk for at least 30 minutes.
3. Combine the flour, pepper, and garlic powder in a bowl.
4. Heat oil in a frying pan.
5. Dredge each chicken piece in the flour mixture and fry until golden brown.
6. Assemble the burgers with the crispy chicken, lettuce, tomato, and mayo.

Alternatives:

- Add pickles or cheese for extra flavor.
- Spice it up with some chili flakes in the flour mix.

3. GFC's Sticky BBQ Wings

Serves: 2

Ingredients:

- 8 chicken wings
- 1 cup BBQ sauce
- 1 cup all-purpose flour
- Salt and pepper to taste
- Vegetable oil for frying

Steps:

1. Season the chicken wings with salt and pepper.
2. Dredge them in flour.
3. Heat the oil in a frying pan and fry the wings until crispy.
4. In a bowl, toss the fried wings with BBQ sauce.
5. Serve immediately with some carrot or celery sticks.

Alternatives:

- For extra heat, mix a dash of hot sauce into the BBQ sauce.
- Try using a honey mustard sauce for a sweet and tangy variation.

Chapter 8

Airfryer Adventures

Crispy Snacks

1. AirFried Crunchy Chicken Strips

Serves: 2

Ingredients:

- 2 chicken breasts, sliced into strips
- 1 cup breadcrumbs
- 1 teaspoon paprika
- 1/2 teaspoon garlic powder
- Salt and pepper to taste
- 1 egg, beaten

Steps:

- Mix breadcrumbs, paprika, garlic powder, salt, and pepper in a bowl.
- Dip chicken strips in beaten egg, then coat with breadcrumb mixture.
- Place in air fryer in a single layer.
- Cook at 200°C (390°F) for 10-12 minutes, turning halfway, until golden and cooked through.

2. Golden Brown Mozzarella Sticks

Serves: 2

Ingredients:

- 1 block of mozzarella cheese (about 200g)
- 1 cup breadcrumbs
- 1/2 teaspoon Italian seasoning
- 1 egg, beaten

Steps:

1. Cut the mozzarella block into approximately 8 even-sized sticks.
2. Freeze the cut mozzarella sticks for at least 1 hour to firm them up and make them easier to handle.
3. In a bowl, mix breadcrumbs with Italian seasoning.
4. Dip each cheese stick first in the beaten egg, ensuring it's fully coated, then roll in the breadcrumb mixture, pressing gently to adhere.
5. Repeat for a double coating: dip again in the egg and then in breadcrumbs. This ensures a crispy crust and less cheese leakage during cooking.
6. Place the coated cheese sticks in the air fryer in a single layer, ensuring they are not touching.
7. Cook at 190°C (375°F) for 6-8 minutes or until golden. Monitor closely to ensure the cheese does not ooze out.
8. Serve hot with your preferred dipping sauce.

Alternatives:

- Dip in marinara sauce or homemade salsa for extra flavor.
- For a spicier kick, mix some chili flakes into the breadcrumb mixture.

3. Zesty Zucchini Fries

Serves: 2

Ingredients:

- 2 zucchinis, cut into sticks
- 1 cup breadcrumbs
- 1/2 teaspoon garlic powder
- 1/2 teaspoon paprika
- Salt and pepper to taste
- 1 egg, beaten

Steps:

1. Mix breadcrumbs with garlic powder, paprika, salt, and pepper.
2. Dip zucchini sticks in egg, then coat with breadcrumb mixture.
3. Place in the air fryer in a single layer.
4. Cook at 200°C (390°F) for 10 minutes, turning halfway, until golden and crispy.

Alternatives:

- Serve with aioli or tzatziki sauce for dipping.

4. AirCrisped Potato Wedges

Serves: 2

Ingredients:

- 2 large potatoes, washed and cut into wedges
- 1 tablespoon olive oil
- 1/2 teaspoon dried rosemary (or your favorite herb mix)
- Salt and pepper to taste

Steps:

1. Toss the potato wedges in olive oil, rosemary, salt, and pepper.
2. Place them in the air fryer in a single layer, ensuring they don't overlap.
3. Cook at 200°C (390°F) for 12-15 minutes, shaking halfway, until golden and crispy.
4. Serve immediately with ketchup or your favorite dipping sauce.

Alternatives:

- For a spicier kick, add a sprinkle of chili powder or paprika.

5. Crunchy AirFried Chickpeas

Serves: 2

Ingredients:

- 1 can chickpeas (drained and rinsed)
- 1 tablespoon olive oil
- 1/2 teaspoon paprika
- 1/2 teaspoon garlic powder
- Salt to taste

Steps:

1. Dry the chickpeas thoroughly using a clean towel.
2. Toss the chickpeas in olive oil, paprika, garlic powder, and salt.
3. Place them in the air fryer in a single layer.
4. Cook at 180°C (355°F) for 12-15 minutes, shaking occasionally, until they're golden and crispy.
5. Serve as a crunchy snack or salad topping.

Alternatives:

- Add a sprinkle of cumin or curry powder for a different flavor profile.

6. AirFryer Stuffed Jalapeños

Serves: 2

Ingredients:

- 6 jalapeños, halved and deseeded
- 100g cream cheese
- 50g cheddar cheese, grated
- 1/2 teaspoon garlic powder
- Salt and pepper to taste
- Breadcrumbs for coating

Steps:

1. In a bowl, mix cream cheese, cheddar cheese, garlic powder, salt, and pepper.
2. Stuff each jalapeño half with the cheese mixture.
3. Dip the stuffed side into breadcrumbs for a light coating.
4. Place them cheese side up in the air fryer.
5. Cook at 190°C (375°F) for 8-10 minutes or until the peppers are tender and the cheese is bubbly and slightly golden.

Alternatives:

- Add some cooked and crumbled bacon to the cheese mixture for extra flavor.

7. AirBaked Apple Chips

Serves: 2

Ingredients:

- 2 apples, thinly sliced (no need to peel)
- 1 teaspoon cinnamon
- 1 tablespoon sugar (optional)

Steps:

1. Mix the apple slices with cinnamon and sugar (if using).
2. Spread them out in the air fryer in a single layer.
3. Cook at 150°C (300°F) for 15-18 minutes, flipping the slices halfway, until they're crispy and golden.
4. Let them cool for a few minutes; they will crisp up further.

Alternatives:

- Drizzle with honey or maple syrup after cooking for a sweet treat.

Main Dishes

1. AirFryer Lemon Herb Chicken

Serves: 2

Ingredients:

- 2 chicken breasts
- 1 tablespoon olive oil
- Zest and juice of 1 lemon
- 1/2 teaspoon dried oregano (or mixed herbs)
- Salt and pepper to taste

Steps:

1. In a bowl, mix olive oil, lemon zest, lemon juice, oregano, salt, and pepper.
2. Marinate the chicken breasts in the mixture for at least 15 minutes.
3. Place the chicken breasts in the air fryer.
4. Cook at 180°C (355°F) for 18-22 minutes or until the internal temperature reaches 75°C (165°F) and the chicken is no longer pink in the center.
5. Let it rest for a few minutes before serving.

Alternatives:

- Serve with a side salad or air fried veggies.

2. Quick AirFryer Pita Pizzas

Serves: 2

Ingredients:

- 2 pita breads
- 4 tablespoons pizza sauce (store-bought or homemade)
- 50g shredded mozzarella
- Toppings of choice: e.g., sliced bell peppers, onions, mushrooms
- 1/2 teaspoon dried Italian seasoning

Steps:

1. Spread 2 tablespoons of pizza sauce on each pita bread.
2. Sprinkle with shredded mozzarella and add your chosen toppings.
3. Season with Italian seasoning.
4. Place the pita pizzas in the air fryer.
5. Cook at 200°C (390°F) for 5-7 minutes or until the cheese is melted and bubbly.
6. Serve immediately.

Alternatives:

- Add pepperoni slices, cooked sausage, or leftover grilled chicken for a meaty version.

3. Airfryer Veggie Frittata

Serves: 2

Ingredients:

- 4 eggs
- 1/4 cup milk
- Salt and pepper to taste
- 1/2 cup mixed veggies (e.g., bell peppers, onions, spinach)
- 2 tablespoons grated cheddar cheese (optional)

Steps:

1. In a bowl, whisk together eggs, milk, salt, and pepper.
2. Stir in the mixed veggies and cheese.
3. Pour the mixture into an air fryer-safe pan or a well-greased oven-safe dish that fits in your air fryer.
4. Cook at 160°C (320°F) for 12-15 minutes or until the frittata is set and slightly golden on top.
5. Let it cool for a minute or two, then slice and serve.

Alternatives:

- Add some chopped cooked bacon or ham for extra protein.

4. AirFried Asian Glazed Meatballs

Serves: 2

Ingredients:

- 200g ground pork or chicken
- 1/4 cup breadcrumbs
- 1 tablespoon soy sauce
- 1 teaspoon ginger paste or finely minced ginger
- 1 garlic clove, minced
- 2 tablespoons sweet chili sauce (for glazing)

Steps:

1. In a bowl, mix the ground meat, breadcrumbs, soy sauce, ginger, and garlic until combined.
2. Form into small meatballs, about the size of a golf ball.
3. Place the meatballs in the air fryer in a single layer.
4. Cook at 180°C (355°F) for 10-12 minutes, shaking halfway, until they are cooked through.
5. Brush the meatballs with sweet chili sauce and cook for an additional 2 minutes.
6. Serve with rice or noodles.

Alternatives:

- For a spicier kick, mix some sriracha into the sweet chili sauce.

5. AirFryer BBQ Chicken Drumsticks

Serves: 2

Ingredients:

- 4 chicken drumsticks
- Salt and pepper to taste
- 1/3 cup BBQ sauce (store-bought or homemade)

Steps:

1. Season the drumsticks with salt and pepper.
2. Place them in the air fryer, ensuring they don't touch each other.
3. Cook at 180°C (355°F) for 20 minutes, turning halfway.
4. Brush the drumsticks with BBQ sauce and cook for another 5-8 minutes until they're caramelized and fully cooked.
5. Serve hot with extra BBQ sauce on the side.

Alternatives:

- Use a spicy BBQ sauce or add a dash of hot sauce for a kick.

6. AirFryer Crispy Tofu Bites

Serves: 2

Ingredients:

- 1 block of firm tofu, pressed and cubed
- 2 tablespoons soy sauce
- 1 tablespoon olive oil
- 1/2 teaspoon garlic powder

Steps:

1. Toss tofu cubes in soy sauce, olive oil, and garlic powder.
2. Place them in a single layer in the air fryer.
3. Cook at 190°C (375°F) for 12-15 minutes, shaking occasionally, until golden and crispy.
4. Serve with a dipping sauce or toss in a stir-fry.

Alternatives:

- Toss the crispy tofu in a sweet chili sauce for an added flavor boost.

7. AirFryer Stuffed Bell Peppers

Serves: 2

Ingredients:

- 2 large bell peppers, any color
- 150g cooked rice
- 100g ground beef or turkey
- 2 tablespoons tomato sauce
- Salt, pepper, and dried herbs to taste
- Grated cheese for topping (optional)

Steps:

1. Cut the tops off the bell peppers and remove the seeds.
2. In a bowl, mix together cooked rice, ground meat, tomato sauce, salt, pepper, and herbs.
3. Stuff each bell pepper with the rice-meat mixture.
4. Place them upright in the air fryer.
5. Cook at 180°C (355°F) for 15 minutes.
6. If using cheese, sprinkle on top and cook for an additional 2-3 minutes until melted.
7. Serve warm.

Alternatives:

- Add some cooked beans or corn to the stuffing mixture for added texture.

8. AirFryer Fish 'n Chips

Serves: 2

Ingredients:

- 2 white fish fillets (like cod or haddock)
- 1/2 cup breadcrumbs
- Salt and pepper to taste
- 2 large potatoes, washed and cut into fries
- 1 tablespoon olive oil

Steps:

1. Season fish fillets with salt and pepper, then coat in breadcrumbs.
2. Toss potato fries in olive oil and a sprinkle of salt.
3. Place the breaded fish and fries in the air fryer, ensuring they don't overlap.
4. Cook at 200°C (390°F) for 12-15 minutes, shaking the fries occasionally, until the fish is cooked through and fries are golden.
5. Serve with tartar sauce or ketchup.

Alternatives:

- Use sweet potato instead of regular potatoes for a different flavor profile.

Veggies & Sides

1. AirFryer Parmesan Zucchini Chips

Serves: 2

Ingredients:

- 1 large zucchini, thinly sliced
- 2 tablespoons grated Parmesan
- 1/2 teaspoon dried basil or oregano (optional)
- Salt and pepper to taste

Steps:

1. Toss zucchini slices in Parmesan, herbs, salt, and pepper.
2. Lay them out in a single layer in the air fryer.
3. Cook at 190°C (375°F) for 8-10 minutes, or until crispy and golden.
4. Serve immediately.

Alternatives:

- For added crunch, you can coat the zucchini in a thin layer of breadcrumbs before cooking.

2. AirFryer Garlic Baby Potatoes

Serves: 2

Ingredients:

- 250g baby potatoes, halved
- 1 tablespoon olive oil
- 2 garlic cloves, minced
- Salt and pepper to taste

Steps:

1. Toss the baby potatoes in olive oil, garlic, salt, and pepper.
2. Spread them in a single layer in the air fryer.
3. Cook at 200°C (390°F) for 15-20 minutes, shaking occasionally, until golden and fork-tender.
4. Serve hot.

Alternatives:

- Sprinkle some grated cheese and chopped herbs just before serving for an extra layer of flavor.

3. AirFryer Asparagus with Lemon Zest

Serves: 2

Ingredients:

- 1 bunch of asparagus, trimmed
- 1 tablespoon olive oil
- Zest of 1 lemon
- Salt and pepper to taste

Steps:

1. Toss the asparagus in olive oil, lemon zest, salt, and pepper.
2. Lay them out in the air fryer in a single layer.
3. Cook at 180°C (355°F) for 8-10 minutes or until tender yet slightly crisp.
4. Serve immediately.

Alternatives:

- Drizzle with a bit of melted butter and crushed garlic for added richness.

4. AirFryer Sweet Corn with Paprika Butter

Serves: 2

Ingredients:

- 2 ears of sweet corn, husked
- 1 tablespoon butter, melted
- 1/4 teaspoon smoked paprika
- Salt to taste

Steps:

1. Brush the corn with melted butter, sprinkle with smoked paprika and salt.
2. Place the corn into the air fryer.
3. Cook at 200°C (390°F) for 12-15 minutes, rotating halfway, until kernels are tender and slightly charred.
4. Serve hot.

Alternatives:

- Sprinkle some grated cheese over the corn just before serving for a cheesy delight.

Chapter 9

Desserts & Treats

Mug Cakes

1. Classic Chocolate Mug Cake

Serves: 1

Ingredients:

- 4 tablespoons all-purpose flour
- 3 tablespoons sugar
- 2 tablespoons cocoa powder
- 3 tablespoons milk
- 2 tablespoons vegetable oil
- A pinch of salt
- 1/4 teaspoon vanilla extract (optional)

Steps:

1. In your mug, whisk together the flour, sugar, cocoa powder, and salt.
2. Add milk, vegetable oil, and vanilla. Mix until smooth.
3. Microwave on high for 90 seconds or until the cake has risen and set.
4. Allow to cool for a few minutes, and then enjoy!

Alternatives:

- Swirl in a spoonful of peanut butter or add a few chocolate chips for added texture.

2. Vanilla Berry Mug Cake

Serves: 1

Ingredients:

- 4 tablespoons all-purpose flour
- 3 tablespoons sugar
- 3 tablespoons milk
- 2 tablespoons vegetable oil
- A pinch of salt
- 1/4 teaspoon vanilla extract
- 2 tablespoons mixed berries (like blueberries or raspberries)

Steps:

1. In your mug, combine the flour, sugar, salt, and vanilla.
2. Add milk and vegetable oil, mixing until smooth.
3. Fold in the berries gently.
4. Microwave on high for about 90 seconds or until the cake has set.
5. Let it cool slightly and enjoy!

Alternatives:

- Use a splash of almond extract instead of vanilla for a different flavor.

No-Bake Cookies

1. Peanut Butter Oat Balls

Serves: 2 (Makes 6-8 balls)

Ingredients:

- 1/2 cup rolled oats
- 1/4 cup peanut butter
- 2 tablespoons honey or maple syrup
- 2 tablespoons raisins or chopped chocolate

Steps:

1. In a bowl, combine all ingredients until they come together.
2. Using your hands, form small balls and place them on a plate.
3. Refrigerate for 1 hour to set.
4. Enjoy straight from the fridge!

Alternatives:

- Add a sprinkle of coconut flakes or some chopped nuts for added crunch.

2. Chocolate Coconut Drops

Serves: 2 (Makes 6-8 drops)

Ingredients:

- 1/4 cup melted chocolate (from chocolate chips or bars)
- 3 tablespoons shredded coconut
- 1 tablespoon chopped nuts (like almonds or walnuts, optional)

Steps:

1. Mix melted chocolate, shredded coconut, and nuts in a bowl.
2. Drop spoonfuls of the mixture onto parchment paper.
3. Chill in the fridge until set, about 30 minutes.
4. Enjoy whenever you need a sweet bite!

Alternatives:

- Swirl in some caramel or peanut butter into the melted chocolate for a different flavor twist.

Fruit Salad Variations

1. Citrus Burst Bowl

Serves: 2

Ingredients:

- 1 grapefruit, segmented
- 2 oranges, segmented
- 1 lemon, juiced and zested
- 2 tablespoons honey
- A pinch of salt

Steps:

1. In a bowl, combine grapefruit and orange segments.
2. In a separate bowl, whisk together lemon juice, zest, honey, and a pinch of salt.
3. Pour the dressing over the citrus fruits and gently toss to combine.
4. Chill and serve.

Alternatives:

- Add thinly sliced fennel for a crunchy, aniseed twist.

2. Melon Medley

Serves: 2

Ingredients:

- 1/2 cup watermelon cubes
- 1/2 cup cantaloupe cubes
- 1/2 cup honeydew cubes
- Juice of 1 lime
- 1 tablespoon chopped fresh mint

Steps:

1. Mix watermelon, cantaloupe, and honeydew cubes in a large bowl.
2. Drizzle with lime juice and sprinkle with chopped mint.
3. Toss gently to mix and serve chilled.

Alternatives:

- Sprinkle some feta cheese on top for a sweet and savory touch.

3. Exotic Fruit Fiesta

Serves: 2

Ingredients:

- 1/2 cup diced pineapple
- 1/2 cup diced mango
- 1/2 cup diced papaya
- 1 passion fruit, pulp scooped out
- 2 tablespoons shredded coconut

Steps:

1. Combine pineapple, mango, and papaya in a bowl.
2. Drizzle over the passion fruit pulp and mix gently.
3. Top with shredded coconut and serve.

Alternatives:

- Drizzle with a bit of honey or maple syrup for added sweetness.

4. Berry Bliss Salad

Serves: 2

Ingredients:

- 1/2 cup strawberries, halved
- 1/2 cup blueberries
- 1/2 cup raspberries
- 1 tablespoon lemon juice
- 1 tablespoon chia seeds

Steps:

1. Combine strawberries, blueberries, and raspberries in a bowl.
2. Drizzle with lemon juice and sprinkle with chia seeds.
3. Toss gently and enjoy!

Alternatives:

- Add a dollop of Greek yogurt on top for creaminess.

5. Pomegranate & Pear Pleasure

Serves: 2

Ingredients:

- Seeds of 1 pomegranate
- 2 pears, diced
- Juice of 1 orange
- 1 tablespoon chopped walnuts

Steps:

1. Mix pomegranate seeds and diced pears in a bowl.
2. Drizzle with fresh orange juice and give it a gentle mix.
3. Garnish with chopped walnuts and serve.

Alternatives:

- Use apple instead of pears for a crunchy variation.

DIY Frozen Yogurt

1. Classic Vanilla Bean Frozen Yogurt

Serves: 2

Ingredients:

- 2 cups plain yogurt (Greek yogurt works best)
- 3 tablespoons honey
- 1 teaspoon pure vanilla extract
- 1 vanilla bean (optional: for added flavor and those black specks)

Steps:

1. Mix yogurt, honey, and vanilla extract in a bowl.
2. If using vanilla bean, split it lengthwise and scrape the seeds. Add seeds to the yogurt mixture.
3. Pour mixture into a shallow dish and freeze for 3-4 hours. Stir every 30 minutes to avoid ice crystal formation.

Alternatives:

- Use maple syrup instead of honey for sweetness.

2. Berry Blast Frozen Yogurt

Serves: 2

Ingredients:

- 2 cups plain yogurt (Greek yogurt works best)
- 1 cup mixed berries (like strawberries, blueberries, raspberries)
- 3 tablespoons honey

Steps:

1. In a blender, blend the mixed berries to a puree.
2. Mix yogurt and honey in a separate bowl.
3. Combine the berry puree with the yogurt mixture.
4. Pour into a shallow dish and freeze, stirring occasionally.

Alternatives:

- Add a dash of lemon juice for a zesty kick.

3. Tropical Mango & Coconut Frozen Yogurt

Serves: 2

Ingredients:

- 2 cups plain yogurt (Greek yogurt works best)
- 1 ripe mango, peeled and pitted
- 3 tablespoons honey
- 2 tablespoons desiccated coconut

Steps:

1. Blend mango into a smooth puree.
2. Combine mango puree, yogurt, honey, and desiccated coconut.
3. Pour the mixture into a dish and freeze, stirring occasionally.

Alternatives:

- Swap mango for pineapple or use both for a tropical blend.

4. Chocolate Swirl Frozen Yogurt

Serves: 2

Ingredients:

- 2 cups plain yogurt (Greek yogurt works best)
- 3 tablespoons cocoa powder
- 3 tablespoons honey
- Chocolate chips or shavings (optional)

Steps:

1. Mix yogurt, cocoa powder, and honey until smooth.
2. If desired, fold in chocolate chips or shavings.
3. Pour into a shallow dish and freeze, giving it a stir now and then.

Alternatives:

- A spoonful of peanut butter blended in can elevate the flavor.

Simple Fruit Crisps

1. Classic Apple Crisp

Serves: 2

Ingredients:

- 2 large apples, peeled, cored, and sliced
- 1 tablespoon granulated sugar
- 1/2 teaspoon cinnamon
- *For the Topping:*
    - 1/2 cup rolled oats
    - 1/4 cup brown sugar
    - 3 tablespoons butter, softened
    - 1/4 teaspoon salt

Steps:

1. Preheat the oven to 375°F (190°C).
2. In a mixing bowl, toss the apple slices with granulated sugar and cinnamon. Transfer to a small baking dish.
3. In another bowl, combine the oats, brown sugar, butter, and salt. Mix until the mixture is crumbly.
4. Sprinkle the oat mixture evenly over the apples.
5. Bake in the preheated oven for about 25 minutes or until the apples are tender and the topping is golden brown.
6. Serve warm.

Alternatives:

- Use pear slices instead of apple or mix both.
- Add a few raisins or dried cranberries to the apple mixture for a twist.

2. Berry Medley Crisp

Serves: 2

Ingredients:

- 2 cups mixed berries (like strawberries, raspberries, blueberries, and blackberries)
- 2 tablespoons granulated sugar
- *For the Topping:*
  - 1/2 cup rolled oats
  - 1/4 cup brown sugar
  - 3 tablespoons butter, softened
  - 1/4 teaspoon salt

Steps:

1. Preheat the oven to 375°F (190°C).
2. In a mixing bowl, toss the mixed berries with granulated sugar. Transfer to a small baking dish.
3. In another bowl, combine the oats, brown sugar, butter, and salt. Mix until the mixture is crumbly.
4. Sprinkle the oat mixture evenly over the berries.
5. Bake in the preheated oven for about 20 minutes or until the berries bubble and the topping turns a nice golden brown.
6. Let it cool slightly before serving.

Alternatives:

- Drizzle a little lemon or orange zest over the berries for an added zing.
- Combine the berries with a sliced banana for a different flavor.

Chapter 10

Budgeting & Shopping Tips

How to Make a Meal Plan

Ever felt the dreaded "what's for dinner" pressure? Planning your meals is like laying out your outfits for the week; it takes away the daily decision fatigue and can save you both time and money. Let's take a journey into the world of meal planning:

Assess Your Week Like a TV Show Schedule: Peek into your upcoming days.

- Prime Time Shows (Busy Days): These are your packed days. Think of them as binge-watching nights where quick recipes or pre-prepared leftovers are your best friends. Perhaps a DIY sandwich night?
- Chill Weekends (Free Days): These are your cooking marathons. Dive deep into a new recipe or craft a dish you've always loved but never had time for.

Choose Your Meals Like Picking Netflix Genres: Diversity is the name of the game.

- Avoid Repetitions: It's like watching a drama series back-to-back. Exciting at first, but it gets old. Had chicken on Monday? Go vegetarian or seafood on Tuesday.
- Dabble in New Releases: Spice up your week with a brand-new recipe. It's like finding a hidden gem in a sea of shows.

The Act of Writing:

- Classic Novels: A whiteboard or notebook in the kitchen feels so personal and tangible.
- Jumping into the Digital Age: Ever heard of Mealime or Yummly? They're like the streaming platforms of meal planning – intuitive, smart, and oh-so-convenient.
- Spreadsheet Saga: For those Excel wizards, think of it as laying out a chessboard. Your moves? Delicious meals for each day.

Smart Shopping: The Adventure Chapter:

- Stick to the Script: It's like going on a treasure hunt with a map. Don't stray and avoid those siren calls of impulse buys.
- Digital Sidekicks: Trusty apps like My Grocery are your compass, always pointing you in the right direction.

Prep's the Prologue to Perfection: The groundwork ensures the story unfolds smoothly.

- Chop in Batches: It's like stockpiling episodes for a binge. After shopping, sort, chop, and store.
- Nightly Prep: Some dishes have a prequel, like marinating. Dive into it the night before to set the stage.

Flexibility: The Plot Twist:

- Switch Scenes: If Tuesday's dish doesn't pan out, slide it to Wednesday. It's your show; you dictate the scenes.
- Emergency Episodes: Always have a couple of backup meals. Think of them as your favorite reruns.

Golden Nuggets of Wisdom:

- Weekly Themes: Think of it as a TV marathon. Dive into "Meatless Monday" or perhaps "Fusion Friday"?
- Poll the Audience: If you've got roommates or family, make it interactive. It's like co-writing a script.
- Seasonal Selections: Embrace what's in season or on sale. It's like catching a movie premiere; timely and exciting.

And Here's a Sneak Peek: Storing food and adjusting serving sizes will be our highlight in upcoming sections. Stick around, and you'll become the Spielberg of meal planning!

Shopping on a Budget: Navigating the Grocery Store Jungle

Embarking on a grocery shopping adventure with limited

funds is a bit like being a contestant on a reality show: you need strategy, awareness, and a bit of charm. But instead of a trophy or cash prize at the end, your reward is a cart full of deliciousness without breaking the bank. Let's dive into this thrilling episode:

The Map of Treasure (or a Shopping List):

- Draft Your Plot: Before stepping into the vast jungle of aisles, scribble down your essentials. It's like a treasure map, ensuring you don't get sidetracked by the shiny, unnecessary stuff.
- Digital Assistance: Platforms like My Grocery or AnyList act like your GPS, ensuring you're on the right path.

Spotting the Diamonds in the Rough (Sales & Discounts):

- Sale Alerts: Sign up for newsletters. It's like receiving a secret code for your next mission.
- Off-brand Adventures: Sometimes the lesser-known paths (or brands) offer the most value. Generic doesn't always mean lower quality; it's just less advertised.

Knowing the Terrain (Seasonal Products):

- Catch of the Day: Focus on what's in season. It's like being at a live concert versus a recorded one – fresher, vibrant, and often cheaper.
- Backstage Passes: Farmers' markets can sometimes grant you VIP access to fresh products without the celebrity price tag.

Strategic Splurging - The Golden Tickets:

- Bulk Buying Binge: Think of non-perishables like a classic movie collection. Buying in bulk might be pricier upfront but offers savings in the long run.
- Quality over Quantity: It's the Oscar-worthy products. Splurging on a good piece of steak or quality olive oil elevates your meal to a blockbuster hit.

Dodging the Pitfalls (Impulse Purchases):

- Stay on Script: Those end-of-aisle displays? They're like trailers – enticing but not always fitting into your main storyline.
- Hunger Games: Shop post-meal. Venturing into the grocery maze on an empty stomach is like facing the villain unarmed.

Golden Nuggets of Wisdom:

- Loyalty is Royalty: Loyalty cards or store memberships can sometimes roll out the red carpet, offering exclusive deals.
- Change the Scene: Alternate between stores. It's like channel surfing, each one might offer a unique show (or deal) worth watching.
- Be an Early Bird or Night Owl: Some stores discount fresh produce at the beginning or end of the day. It's like catching the pre-show or after-party.

Final Credits: Remember, every shopping trip is an episode in your culinary series. Some will be blockbuster hits, others learning curves. But each one crafts your journey to becoming a budgeting superstar! ✻

Seasonal Shopping: The UK's Orchestra of Harvests

Imagine the changing seasons in the UK as an evolving orchestral piece. Each movement (or season) introduces new instruments (fruits, veggies, and other produce), resonating with distinct notes, melodies, and rhythms, awaiting their solo. By tuning into this melody, you can dance your way to budget-friendly, flavourful, and nutrition-packed meals. So, how can you align your shopping spree with Britain's symphony of harvests? Here's your guide:

The Concert Programme (Seasonal Charts):

- Nature's Symphony: Just as concert-goers peek at the programme to know the sequence, grab a UK-specific seasonal produce chart. This shows what's in crescendo this month.
- Tech's Playlist: Apps or sites like Eat Seasonably or the BBC Good Food Seasonality Table keep you updated on the UK's fresh picks.

VIP Passes (Farmers' Markets):

- Meeting the Maestros: Buying directly from British growers is like having a backstage chat with the maestro. Absolute freshness and stories of the soil guaranteed.
- Curtain Call Deals: Visiting during the market's closing hours might score you encore deals as vendors wrap up.

Auditions (Selecting the Best):

- Freshness Takes the Stage: Feel, sniff, and at times

sample. Opt for firm, colourful, and fragrant produce. Like choosing the lead violinist based on their audition.
- Avoid the Out-of-Tune: Overripe or bruised items often come with a discount. Perfect for immediate jams or purees.

Bulk Buys: The Showstopper:

- Season's Hits: When the likes of British strawberries or Kentish apples are in season and priced lower, it's time to hoard. It's like securing tickets for every performance of a hit show.
- Preservation Act: Brush up on pickling or freezing techniques. A bit like recording your favourite concert to replay later.

Setting the Stage (Storing):

- Staging it Right: Store your British produce in the best conditions. Remember, not all fruits and veggies like to be stored together; some may accelerate the ripening of others.

Encore: As an example, in the chilly embrace of a British winter, think Brussels sprouts, leeks, and parsnips. Come spring, the melody changes to the soft notes of asparagus and the brightness of early strawberries. Summer brings the full chorus with berries, cherries, and courgettes, while autumn closes the concert with plums, apples, and pumpkins. Tune in to this rhythm and make the most of the UK's bounty!

Storing Food Correctly: The Art of the Culinary Librarian

Picture this: Your kitchen is like an enormous library, and every food item is a precious book. Just as you wouldn't leave a rare manuscript out in the sun, you wouldn't want to let your fresh veggies wilt away in the wrong part of your fridge. And, just like certain genres have their specific sections, your foods have their optimal storage spots. How then, dear librarian of the larder, can you ensure each 'book' is properly preserved? Here's your guide:

Shelving Systems (Your Fridge & Freezer):

- Top Shelf Reads: Items that don't need cooking, like deli meats or leftovers, go on the top fridge shelf. Think of them as your 'currently reading' pile, ready for quick access.
- Drawer Drama: These humidity-controlled sections are like the reserved seats of a theatre, specifically designed for fruits and vegetables.
- Door Deals: The fridge door is the warmest part, suitable for items that can withstand slight temperature variations. Condiments, juices, and sauces? They're your paperback novels.

Canned Chronicles (The Pantry):

- Dark Tales: Pantries should be cool, dry, and dark. Think of it as the historical fiction section – ideal for grains, spices, and canned goods.
- Serial Sequels: Store items used frequently, like cooking oils or cereal, at eye level. Much like your favourite book series that you'd want at arm's reach.

Countertop Collections:

- Solo Novels: Some fruits, like bananas, emit gases that can ripen (and eventually rot) other produce. Keep them isolated, much like that stand-alone novel that doesn't fit into a series.
- Epic Sagas: Items like potatoes and onions are best kept in a cool, dark place but not in the fridge. Think of them as the epic sagas that demand a separate corner.

Temperature Tales:

- Chilled Thrillers: Meat, fish, and dairy products? They require the coldest part of your fridge, usually the bottom. Think of them as your thrillers, best kept in a chilling environment.
- Warm Reads: Room temperature is best for some veggies, like tomatoes, as the cold can affect their texture and taste. They're like cozy mystery novels, best enjoyed outside of the chilling fridge section.

Expiration Expositions:

- Timely Check-outs: Regularly check expiry dates. Consumables past their prime? They're like borrowed library books – they need to go before you face any penalties!

Closing Notes: Just as some books demand careful handling and specific storage conditions, so do your food items. By mastering the art of culinary storage, you ensure that every chapter of your meal is fresh, tasty, and free of any plot twists (read: unexpected mould or wilt). Happy 'reading' and eating!

Chapter 11

Scaling & Meal Prepping

Solo **Suppers:** Cooking for one isn't just about satisfying immediate hunger; it's a chance to indulge in personal tastes and perhaps, create a meal for now and another for later.

1. Personalised Plates: Tailor everything to your preference. Fancy some extra spice? Go ahead. Detest broccoli? Skip it.
2. Divide and Conquer: Many recipes cater to families. If a dish serves four, quarter the ingredients. Or better yet, make the full portion and save leftovers for subsequent meals.
3. Leftover Luxuries: Think of the future! Leftovers from a dinner can metamorphose into tomorrow's lunch or even the next dinner. Store them appropriately, and they'll be a treat when reheated.

Dynamic Duo Dining: When you're cooking for two, perhaps with a flatmate or partner, you're not just feeding—

you're creating shared memories.

1. Double the Fun: Most single-serving recipes can be effortlessly doubled. Simply multiply ingredients by two.
2. Taste Fusion: Understand your dining partner's likes and dislikes. It ensures shared meals are a pleasure for both.
3. Bonus Bites: Cooking for two often leads to some leftovers. These can be perfect for those late-night study sessions or quick lunches.

Group Gatherings: Cooking for more, like a study group or friends, presents an opportunity to be the host with the most while also thinking ahead.

1. Bulk Benefits: When cooking for a group, bulk buying becomes your best friend. It's cost-effective and ensures there's plenty to go around.
2. Online Assist: Use recipe scaling tools to adjust for larger groups. It simplifies the maths and helps you get quantities right.
3. Leftover Love: The beauty of group cooking? Plenty of leftovers. Store them efficiently, and you've got meals ready for days when you're too busy or tired to cook.

Whether you're dining solo, with a partner, or hosting a feast, scaling recipes is a skill you'll cherish. And remember, the joy of cooking isn't just in the eating but also in the anticipation of the next delicious meal. So, go on, make extra, and relish the convenience and taste of your creations over and over again!

Freezing and Reheating 101: Maximising Meal Potential

In the culinary world, the freezer can be a student's best ally. It's like a time machine for your food. Imagine making a scrumptious dish today and enjoying it two weeks from now, as fresh as the day you cooked it. But, as with any superpower, there are rules to follow. Let's explore the do's and don'ts of freezing and reheating.

Freezing Fundamentals:

1. Cool Before You Freeze: Always let your freshly cooked meals cool down to room temperature before freezing. This prevents the formation of ice crystals that can ruin the texture of the food.
2. Portion Control: Freeze meals in individual portions. It's quicker to thaw, and you won't have to defrost more than you need.
3. Label Love: Use a marker to note down the date and dish name on the container. You'd be surprised how similar everything looks once frozen.
4. Air is the Enemy: Try to remove as much air as possible from bags or containers. Air can lead to freezer burn, which can severely degrade the quality of your food.
5. Short and Sweet: While freezing extends the life of food, it's not infinite. As a rule of thumb, most cooked meals maintain their quality for up to 3 months in the freezer.

Reheating Rules:

1. Patience Pays: Ideally, transfer food from the freezer

to the fridge 24 hours before you plan to eat it. Slow thawing preserves flavour and texture.
2. Microwave Magic: If you're using a microwave, always cover your food and use the defrost setting first. Then, microwave on the regular setting in bursts, stirring in between to ensure even reheating.
3. Oven Options: When reheating in an oven, cover the dish with foil to prevent it from drying out. It may take a bit longer than the microwave, but it's perfect for dishes like casseroles or pies.
4. Safety First: Always ensure reheated food reaches a temperature of at least 74°C (165°F). A simple kitchen thermometer can be a valuable tool for this.
5. One and Done: Never refreeze something you've already thawed and reheated. It's not just a matter of taste but safety.

In a Nutshell: The art of freezing and reheating can make your culinary life as a student both convenient and cost-effective. By following these guidelines, you can ensure your dishes maintain their quality, flavour, and safety, allowing you to enjoy your kitchen creations anytime the craving strikes!

The Reheat Rundown: Dos, Don'ts, and Precautions

Navigating the world of reheating is a bit like prepping for an exam. You've got the facts that never change, some tricky questions you need to navigate with care, and the golden nuggets you always get right. Let's break it down.

Never Reheat These:
1. Rice: Believe it or not, rice can be a hotbed for

bacteria if not handled properly. Always cool rice quickly after cooking and store it in the fridge. When reheating, ensure it's piping hot throughout, but only reheat once.
2. Eggs: Avoid reheating eggs at all costs. That rubbery texture? It's a sign they've been cooked twice, and they could become toxic.
3. Spinach and Beets: Upon reheating, these vegetables can convert their nitrates into nitrites and other harmful compounds. Best enjoyed fresh!
4. Seafood: Delicate and easily spoiled, seafood can become risky territory if reheated. Especially if it wasn't stored correctly after the first round of cooking.

Reheat with Precaution:

1. Chicken: Reheating chicken multiple times isn't just a flavor no-no; it's a health risk. Always ensure chicken is reheated thoroughly and let it stand for a few minutes before eating. Only give it a second chance once!
2. Potatoes: Always refrigerate cooked potatoes promptly. If you decide to reheat them, ensure they're steaming hot all the way through.
3. Pasta: When reheating pasta, especially ones with sauces, sprinkle some water or broth to keep them from drying out. Microwave in short bursts and stir in between.
4. Soups and Stews: Always reheat to a rolling boil and stir frequently to ensure even heat distribution.

Top Tip: Trust your senses! If something smells or looks off, it's always better to be safe than sorry. Plus, no one needs a surprise food poisoning episode right before a big exam.

Remember, reheating foods can be as easy as ABC, as long as you're aware of the dos and don'ts. Keep these golden rules in mind, and you'll be set for many warm and delicious meals ahead!

Batch Cooking Brilliance: A Crash Course in Culinary Efficiency

Remember the feeling of having an extra set of lecture notes during revision week? That's batch cooking for your kitchen. It's like preparing for an exam well in advance, so when the hunger pangs hit, you're not scrambling for answers (or in this case, recipes). Let's dive into how you can apply the genius of batch cooking to your student life.

1. The Basics of Batch Cooking: Imagine spending a Sunday afternoon cooking, and by evening, you have meals lined up for the entire week. Batch cooking is all about efficiency, making multiple meals in one go. It's the Netflix binge-session of the cooking world; once you start, you just can't stop!
2. The Bulk Buy Bonanza: Venture into the world of wholesale stores or bulk buy sections. Not only do they save pennies (essential for that student budget), but they're the backbone of a successful batch cooking session.
3. Variety, Variety, Variety: Think of batch cooking like your Spotify playlist. You wouldn't want to listen to the same song on repeat, right? Similarly, cook up a medley of dishes, so you have a different

tune (or taste) for each day of the week.

4. Freezer Friends: Your freezer is about to become your new best mate. Invest in some good-quality freezer containers. They'll hold onto your culinary masterpieces, ensuring they're as fresh and delicious days (or even weeks) later as they were when you first made them.

5. Schedule and Strategize: Got a particularly busy week? Or perhaps a week where you're feeling lazy? Plan your batch cooking sessions around your academic and social calendar. And hey, why not make it a social event? Get your flatmates involved, put on some tunes, and make a fun afternoon of it!

Top Tip: When venturing into batch cooking, always label your dishes with dates. It's easy to forget when you made that lasagna or curry. A simple label can ensure you're eating dishes while they're at their prime. Plus, it'll save you from the sniff test – you know the one!

In the world of student living, where deadlines, lectures, and social commitments jostle for space, batch cooking can be your secret weapon. It's not just about food; it's about reclaiming a little peace of mind, one bulk-cooked meal at a time. Happy cooking!

If you've reached this page, it means you've embarked on a journey through the tantalizing and practical world of cooking as a student. Congratulations! From simple breakfasts to weekend specials, you've explored a diverse menu of options tailored just for you. But remember, this is merely the beginning.

While this guide is crafted to ease your way into the kitchen, it is by no means the end of the road. In fact, think of it as your very first recipe card in a vast collection waiting to be assembled by you. Cooking, much like life, is about experimentation, learning, and growth. Some days, your dishes might resemble a Michelin-star masterpiece, and on others, they may seem like a 'Kitchen Nightmare'. But every mistake, every burnt toast, and over-salted pasta, is a stepping stone towards becoming a better cook.

Let your curiosity lead the way. Don't be afraid to swap ingredients, try new flavors, or invent an entirely new dish. Remember, the greatest dishes in history weren't born from following recipes to the T, but by daring to be different.

The kitchen is more than just a place to cook; it's a space where memories are made, traditions are passed down, and creativity knows no bounds. Share your food with friends, celebrate small victories, and always eat dessert (especially if it's a mug cake).

Lastly, remember why you started this journey. Whether to save money, eat healthier, impress someone, or just for the sheer love of food, hold on to that reason. Let it drive you, motivate you, and above all, let it remind you of the joys and wonders of cooking.

Here's to many more meals, memories, and culinary adventures! Now, put on that apron, and let the magic begin. Happy cooking!

Appendices

Nutritional Guidelines: Building Blocks for a Balanced Diet

Embarking on your culinary journey is exhilarating, but it's equally important to ensure you're getting the nutrients your body craves. Especially during your student years, when your brain is in overdrive, and your body is constantly on the move. Here's a concise guide:

1. Carbohydrates: They're your body's primary energy source. Aim for whole grains like brown rice, quinoa, and oats. They release energy slowly, keeping you full and fueled for longer.
2. Proteins: Think of them as your body's building blocks. Whether you're a carnivore, vegetarian, or somewhere in between, there's a protein source for everyone. Chicken, fish, tofu, legumes, and eggs are just a few examples.
3. Fats: Essential for hormone production and vitamin absorption. Olive oil, avocados, nuts, and fatty fish are great sources of healthy fats.
4. Vitamins & Minerals: These micronutrients play a plethora of roles, from bone health to boosting your immune system. Incorporate a rainbow of fruits and

veggies to cover all your bases.

5. Hydration: Remember, about 60% of your body is water! Aim to drink at least 8 glasses a day, more if you're active.

Tip: Moderation is key! It's okay to indulge occasionally, but balance it out with nutritious meals most of the time.

Glossary: Decoding Cooking Lingo

Venturing into the kitchen might feel like entering a new world, filled with strange terms and rituals. Worry not! Here's your trusty guide to making sense of it all:

- Al Dente: An Italian term meaning "to the tooth." It refers to cooking pasta so it's still firm when bitten.
- Blanch: Briefly plunging veggies into boiling water, then immediately into cold water. Helps retain color and crunch.
- Deglaze: Pouring a liquid (often wine or broth) into a pan to lift the browned bits off the bottom. Adds flavor to sauces and stews.
- Julienne: Cutting veggies into thin, matchstick-like strips.
- Mirepoix: A French term for the trio of chopped onions, carrots, and celery, often used as a base in many dishes.
- Braise: Slow-cooking method where the food is partially submerged in liquid, often used for tough cuts of meat to make them tender.
- Fold: A gentle mixing method, often used to

incorporate airy ingredients (like whipped cream) without deflating them.
- Sear: Cooking the surface of meat at high heat until a brown crust forms. Locks in flavors and juices.
- Zest: The outermost layer of citrus fruits. Packed with aromatic oils, it adds a burst of flavor.
- Roux: A mixture of flour and fat, often used as a thickening agent for sauces and soups.
- Poach: Cooking food gently in liquid, just below boiling point. Commonly used for eggs and fish.
- Sauté: Cooking food quickly in a pan over high heat with a small amount of oil.
- Simmer: Cooking liquid just below the boiling point, where small bubbles form but don't burst to the surface.
- Caramelize: Slowly cooking sugar or foods with natural sugars (like onions) until they become brown and develop a sweet, deep flavor.
- Dredge: Coating food, often meat or fish, in flour or breadcrumbs before cooking.
- Broil: Cooking food directly under a heat source, often used to brown the top of dishes.
- Parboil: Partially boiling food, so it's partially cooked. It's often followed by another cooking method.
- Chiffonade: Slicing leafy vegetables or herbs into thin strips.

Tip: Cooking lingo might seem complex initially, but as you experiment and practice, these terms will become second nature. Dive in, and soon you'll be speaking the kitchen language fluently!

Substitution Chart: Swapping in a Pinch

Cooking often requires improvisation, especially when the cupboard springs a surprise (or lack thereof). Here's a list to arm you with some backup plans:

- Buttermilk: 1 cup milk + 1 tbsp lemon juice or white vinegar. Let sit for 5 minutes.
- Honey: Equal amounts of maple syrup, agave nectar, or even molasses.
- Bread Crumbs: Crushed crackers, rolled oats, or even cornflakes for a crunchier coat.
- Sour Cream or Yogurt: Equal amounts of mashed avocado, pureed cottage cheese, or silken tofu.
- Wine (in cooking): Broth with a splash of vinegar or lemon juice for acidity. If it's red wine you're missing, a bit of grape or pomegranate juice can work too.
- Fresh Herbs: Generally, use 1/3 the amount of dried herbs. For example, 1 tbsp fresh basil = 1 tsp dried basil.
- Eggs (in baking): For one egg, substitute with a half mashed banana, 1/4 cup applesauce, or a mixture of 1 tbsp flaxseed with 2.5 tbsp water. Let the flaxseed

mixture sit for a few minutes to thicken.
- Butter: In most recipes, unsweetened applesauce, mashed bananas, or even avocado puree can do the trick.
- Chocolate (unsweetened): 3 tablespoons of unsweetened cocoa powder + 1 tablespoon of butter or oil for every ounce of unsweetened chocolate.
- Lemon Juice: Equal amounts of white vinegar or lime juice.
- Cornstarch (for thickening): Use twice the amount of all-purpose flour.
- Garlic Clove: 1/2 teaspoon of garlic powder or 1/8 teaspoon of granulated garlic.
- Brown Sugar: Equal amounts of white sugar mixed with molasses. For 1 cup of brown sugar, use 1 cup of white sugar and 1-2 tablespoons of molasses.
- Mayonnaise (in salads and cold recipes): Use an equal amount of yogurt, mashed avocado, or sour cream.
- Baking Powder: For 1 teaspoon, use 1/4 teaspoon baking soda + 1/2 teaspoon cream of tartar.
- Baking Soda: For 1 teaspoon, use 3 teaspoons of baking powder (although this might affect the final texture).
- Molasses: Honey, dark corn syrup, or maple syrup can be used in equal amounts.
- Ricotta Cheese: Cottage cheese or mashed tofu can often fill in seamlessly, especially in pasta dishes.
- Whole Milk: Half & half or a blend of equal parts skim milk and cream.
- Cream of Tartar (in whipping egg whites): For every 1/8 teaspoon, use 1/2 teaspoon of white vinegar or

lemon juice.
- Cocoa Powder (unsweetened): Melted unsweetened chocolate (adjust fat and sugar accordingly).
- Red Pepper Flakes: A dash of hot sauce can provide that kick, though be mindful of the liquid content.
- Vanilla Extract: Equal amounts of maple syrup, brandy, or rum.
- Mascarpone Cheese: Blend equal parts of softened cream cheese and whipping cream.
- Fresh Milk (in baking): For 1 cup, substitute with 1/2 cup evaporated milk + 1/2 cup water.
- Light Corn Syrup: Equal amounts of honey or a sugar-water solution.
- Mustard (in recipes): For 1 tablespoon, use 1 tablespoon dried mustard + 1 teaspoon water, 1 teaspoon vinegar, and 1 teaspoon sugar.
- Oil (in baking): Applesauce or fruit purees can often replace half the oil in baking recipes.
- Yeast: For 1 packet (or 2 1/4 teaspoons) of active dry yeast, use 1 cup of double-fermented sourdough starter. Remember to adjust the rising time accordingly.
- Worcestershire Sauce: For 1 tablespoon, combine 1 tablespoon soy sauce, 1 pinch sugar, and a dash of lemon juice.

Tip: Always be cautious about proportions and taste-test when you're substituting, especially in baking. A slight alteration can give you a completely new flavor profile, which might be your next favorite thing! Your culinary journey is all about creativity, exploration, and, most importantly, enjoying the process.

BNW
PUBLISH

Join us on your favourite platform, Scan the QR code on your phone or tablet

Printed in Great Britain
by Amazon